Patrick Joseph McCall

Irish Nóiníns

Being a collection of I. Historical poems and ballads, II. Translations from

the Gaelic, III. Humorous and characteristic sketches, IV. Miscellaneous

songs

Patrick Joseph McCall

Irish Nóiníns
Being a collection of I. Historical poems and ballads, II. Translations from the Gaelic,
III. Humorous and characteristic sketches, IV. Miscellaneous songs

ISBN/EAN: 9783744779531

Printed in Europe, USA, Canada, Australia, Japan

Cover: Foto ©Thomas Meinert / pixelio.de

More available books at **www.hansebooks.com**

(DAISIES)

BEING A COLLECTION OF

I.—Historical Poems and Ballads.

II.—Translations from the Gaelic.

III.—Humorous and Characteristic Sketches.

IV.—Miscellaneous Songs.

BY

PATRICK JOSEPH McCALL

(CAVELLUS).

DUBLIN:

SEALY, BRYERS AND WALKER

(A. T. & C., L.),

94, 95 & 96 MIDDLE ABBEY STREET.

1894.

PATRICK JOSEPH McCALL

BRADY, BYERS AND WALKER

CONTENTS.

Humorous and Characteristic Sketches.

Miscellaneous Songs.

IRISH NÓINÍNS.*
(DAISIES.)

Far o'er the field, like sunlets, see
The myriad daisies shine,
'Neath silvern lids tipped blushingly
Peep out their golden eyne ;
These dearest of all flowers I love
For meek-eyed modesty —
My sweet, sweet nóiníns—Irish nóiníns—
Charm the heart of me !

From every skaugh and drinan down †
The birdlings pipe their lay,
Flossy each breast, all bright and brown,
That hides the heart so gay ;
Dear are these wingéd minstrels all,
But wren-birds, wild and wee—
The sweet, sweet dreóilíns—Irish nóiníns—
Charm the heart of me !

---

* Pronounced Noan-yeens. Some Gaelic words in the above require elucidation. Thus, Dreóilíns (Droal-yeens), wrens ; Paistíns (Pausth-yeens), children ; Danins (Daun-yeens), songs.

† Skaugh, a white thorn ; Drinan down, the black (brown) thorn or sloe.

Adown the meadow, freckle-faced,
　　The laughing children run :
Long by the marshpools have they chased
　　The dragon-flies i' the sun.
Light every heart, bright every eye,
　　And cherub-like their glee—
These sweet, sweet páistíns—Irish nóiníns—
　　Charm the heart of me !

Now, with twin twinkling, fairy feet,
　　A maiden goes the path—
Fair is her face, divinely sweet,
　　Her voice soft music hath ;
So delicately, so gracefully,
　　She trips across the lea—
Our sweet, sweet, cáilíns—Irish nóiníns—
　　Charm the heart of me !

Lo, in my hand I hold a book
　　To soothe my soul with song,
Here, in this still, sequestered nook,
　　I read it, lingering long :
Each lay therein as raindrops pure,
　　Soft as the mead-winds free—
These sweet, sweet dáníns—Irish nóiníns—
　　Charm the heart of me !

For aye may every Irish face
  With truth's pure halo glow,
That nóinín garlands we may place
  On each unsullied brow.
Never such faithful ones ought leave
  Poor Ireland while unfree,
But cling like nóiníns—Irish nóiníns—
  Here so dear to me!

IRISH NÓINÍNS.

Historical Poems and Ballads.

GLEN SCONE.

(A STONE GRAVER'S SONG.)

["The grave of Queen Scota is to be seen between Sliev
Mish and the sea, near Tralee."—*Annals of the Four Masters.*]

"I mount the unheaved pillar stone,
 Beside the blue slate, earthwise, laid.
The mourners, to the brook, have gone,
 To edge, again, their hewing blade.
I, here, behind, in green Glen Scone,
 Work at my facet-scoring trade;
And form those signs of lore, unknown,
 Amergin gave—bead, notch, and braid!"—
Tap, tap, tap, tap!—a cross-grained rock
Resists the flint and mallet shock.

" I knock, but do not wake the Queen,
    Who stands beneath, facing the East—
Stern guardian, armed with helve and skian,
    Her gold snake torque upon her breast;
Her banner, for a mantling screen,
    Enfolds her chilly house of rest—
Here, came the six sons, yestere'en,
    Their dead one bearing, raven-tressed."—
Tap, tap, tap, tap!—with measured blow,
He 'graves the name of her, below.

"They came: Amergin dropped a tear,
    As hot as battle's fever blood ;
But never one shed haughty Ir,
    As by the yawning pit he stood;
Chafed Heber Finn, beneath her bier,
    And cursed her slayers, in his mood ;
While Heber Donn, like wounded deer,
    Slunk, restless, to the green-topped wood!"--
Tap, tap, tap, tap!—four uncial spears
Glance Easternwards—a sign appears!

"Long, Heremon mused, grave and wise—
    His mother's darling counterpart.
She gave to him the dove's mild eyes—
    A father's gift, his eagle's heart!
Young Colpa mewed, with catlike cries,
    That almost rent the oaks apart,

As on them sprang his piercing sighs,
   Rebounding o'er the woody scart!"—
Tap, tap, tap, tap!—four hostile lines
He cuts—a second cryptic shines!

"Yet, they stood there, a conquering band
   Of their bright Isle of Destiny!
How wond'rous green, this western land,
   Of lavish grass and laden tree!
Ours now!—here, undismayed, we stand,
   Masters of it, from sea to sea,
Won by thy wand, won by thy hand,
   Won, sleeping Mother Queen, by thee!"—
Tap, tap, tap, tap!—two notches scar
The edge—a third Rune-character!

"Alas, we lost thee, Queen! Thy fall
   Was grievous for us at Glen Scone,
Where we have tombed thee!—Very tall,
   Blue ribbed, will rise thy dallan stone,
Higher than I, erect—a spall
   As tough, scarce has my graver known,
Save one—the crystal Lia Fál,
   I carved for Lewy's turgid throne!"—
Tap, tap, tap, tap!—three lances stretched
With westering points—a fourth is etched!

" I strike; joint-rigid grows my hand,
    Smiting, that holds the mauling heft;
Strained every sinew, nerve, and strand,
    The flint point guiding, with my left!
For ages must this pillar stand,
    Carved with its Oghams, deep and deft,
Writ first by gods of sea and land
    In stony books of cave and cleft!"—
Tap, tap, tap, tap!—one short broad line,
An arris notch—the last quaint sign!

" Soon ready, now! Comes Heremon,
    Pacing the path the mourners made,
With him, the Druids' favourite one,
    Amergin, reft and disarrayed!
Soon will my graving task be done—
    Soon shall the pillar, high be laid;
And the exploring, curious sun,
    Its mystic passages invade!"—
Tap, tap, tap, tap!—six carven rings
Crown her—dead mother of six kings!

DUBHTACH MAC UI LUGAIR'S DEATH-SONG.

[Dubhtach Mac Ui Lugair (pronounced Du-uch Magilligur)
was Ard Filea, or chief Bard of Erinn, during the reign of
Ard Righ Lairy (Laoghaire), and was St. Patrick's first con-
vert at Tara. After Lairy's death, Dubhtach resided with
Creevan (Crimthan), King of Hy-Kinsella, A.D. 484.]

Is it the king who calls, who gracious gives
A gold cup, brimming meadful, and who liefs
A lay?—Ah, generous king! my voice grows faint;
My heart and harp, alike, have crust and taint
Of rheumy night, that rot the chords of song,
 And numb the strings of life!—Your hoary bard
 Feels age's cooling dews his heart ensward;
Feels his bill-nestling song birds, silent, long
For bonds of pleasant slumber, fast and strong!

Yet, shall he wake a bird of ruddy breast,
For this, his evening song; whose voice is best
Attuned to simple melody—to Hope,
 To Truth, to Love, three master-keys,
That swiftly ope
 Song's tabernacled mysteries!

A prelude, daltha, play !—the air we heard
  Together, 'neath the cromlech of Mac Lir,
  One balmy summer twilight, yester-year—
A Danaun tuning, weird,
  Of soothing sweep; like sound of water-strings
From cascade of the Brugh, as high it flings
A spray of sleep on all who linger near :
Strangely it lulled me, pouring on my ear
  A flood, like early cradle-comfortings !

I, Dubhtach, dying, praise you, monarch meek !—
Creevan, my liege, the comely son of Fiac !
A flaming torch o'er battle's murky pall !
A shining sun in pleasure's banquet hall !
A heart of molten gold in bower of love !
A serpent's knot, untied, in wisdom's grove !

I, dying, praise you, twice ! At Bresal's rath,
  God be my witness !—direly wounding Gael !—
I saw you like a bull, make many a path,
  Through moving trees of spears and rocks of mail ;
For I was there to note. My eagle's eyes,
Now filmed as owl's, saw my king's victories !

I, dying, praise you, thrice. I saw you go,
Like sun, that wades through sheeting clouds of
  snow—

Go through the swathing Suir, when brimmed its
    banks,
When rose the river to your horse's flanks!—
God's truth, my tale!—Saw you Cnoc Ainé win—
God's truth, again!—At Saur, and at Magh Finn,
Victorious. With memory of your deeds,
O Creevan, rise my tears, like gathering beads
Of dew, o'er Liffey's plain! . . .
For I shall never see a fray again!

Dying, I praise my king—a wolf in war,
In peace, your heart grew mild, as evening star,
Alit, with twinkling joy and kindliness:
So 'twas, when holy Patrick came to bless
Your brow and mine, and you, the king, believed,
And I, the bard! Since then, we've never grieved
For hostings, cattle-forays and the flow
Of sating blood—false thirsts of long ago,
For you and me! . . .
Christ's Blood, shed for us, brought satiety.

Chief Seer of Erinn, I. My lore-lamp shone
O'er Tara, Lugair's first and poet son!
Once, I remember, Ard Righ Lairy sought
My subtle counsel; vainly, him I taught
The truth—a wretched king, who would not bend
A knee to God, for me, his dearest friend;

Nor crook a neck, although his heart I won,
  By patient pleading: so, he stubborn, went
  Unsaved, to God's subduing punishment—
Proud son of haughty Nial—his father's son!

God's fingers early touched me: pricked my sloth,
  A minstrel's fatal fault!—I journeyed wide—
At all the sinful ways of mankind wroth!—
O'er Erinn of the Streams: by peak and plain,
By lake and cliff, I went, and many a fane
  And cross I raised, to Him, our Crucified!

Ah, once, the old war fire consumed my zeal!—
Do you remember, king, whose loon of steel,
Whose loric, cloak, and bronzen buttoned shield,
You wore at Ocha, panting on the field?
  Mine, noble king! 'Twas there, that eight score fell,
And ten, by your right hand. Your father broke
Full twelve prime battles: four, your waxing stroke;
Till Patrick vexéd came, and stilled your hand;
And changed my battle-song, and soothed the land,
  With crozier, cross, and bell!

My life knew bliss of love!—the white armed Mel,
  The beautiful of face, the fleet of foot,
  The fragrant apple tree of bending fruit,
I saw and sighed for; and my pleading fell
On gracious ears. My Queen of Beauty gave

Sweet love and courtship to me, soft as wave
That folds the shore! . . .
My Mel, my Beautiful, is now no more.

I sang my songs of Truth: my fame spread wide,
Like conch, flung in a lake's cliff-margined tide,
Concircling long with foam-bursts; so, my shell
Of song, within my heart, heaved many a bell
Of music, rippling far, till came my meed—
A poet's from a king!—a comely steed
Of chequered lawn and loam, bee-humming rills,
And slow-waved shore: thrice humped with echoing
    hills—
Torchar, Formal, and Fordrum!—whose long tail
Is lashed by Bana, mingling sand and shale;
Whose mouth, the loud-resounding ocean laves,
Where, whinnying, come white-crested maney waves,
Sea mares, to woo him; twice, they course each day,
From pebbly, shell-paved stables, far away.

I, dying, praise you, king! your gift, this land,
Stretching from plume of hill to hem of strand,
Horse-like in form—a royal prize for song!
Fleeting as fair, I shall not hold it long,
Though all the Courts of Heaven, nine, and one
Of Earth—gold Croghan's mountain throne,
Your pledge for it!—what pledge have I, for life?
Had I, for more than life or land—my wife?—

B

For Mel, my Beautiful, is dead, these years . . .
Again, my tears.

O monarch, music-loving! patience, now,
I faint and tire; death drops, upon my brow,
Like whortle berries rise; my cheek pales white,
And I will cease the strain; for, in the night,
All birds are silent! ..   Lead me in, dear page.
A strange hand-union ours, of youth and age:
You think of mossy springs of life and love;
I, of their slimy mouths, in sea-girt grove,
Where rocks a corach, on an ebbing tide,
To bear me to Sen Patrick—and my bride!

CLONTARF.

A NORDLAND LAMENT.

[ARGUMENT—Hako, a Scandinavian scald or poet, one day
discovers his little son poring over the account of the battle of
Clontarf, as given in the *Nial Sagas*, or Scaldic chronicles of
Scandinavia. The poet thus addresses the boy. Some
allusions therein to Northern mythology require explanation
—thus: Odin is the Northern Jupiter; Thor (The Thunderer),
Mars; the Valkyriors are Odin's angels of death; Valhalla is
the paradise of those who die in battle, while Nifleimir is the
future abode of those who die peaceful deaths; Lok, or Loki,
is the ruler of the darker nether world; Hela is his daughter.]

Hide that page, my little prying Dane,
Clasped within its horn-leaved tome again;
For the story there, which darkling lies
Suits not you, but one grown old and wise—
One with patient, quiet eyes!

There, in Scaldic runes is redly writ—
Cold the trembling hand which pencilled it!
Cluain-Tarav's tale—O lurid leaf!
Once, my child, my own eyes, wet with grief
Through it passaged fugitive.

Once, that little once—in suns gone by,
One song hushed and solemn evening, I,
Fearful of my absent father's frown,
Took this very same Nial Saga down,
With bronze clasp and cover brown

Woe with woe! reading, my Nordland pride
Sank within my heart, that twilight-tide;
As a-past, on Fancy's wind-fleet wing,
I beheld that clay-sweet morn of spring—
Its blood fetid evening!

Seeing there, the dark Valkyrior brood
Weaving shrouds with Danish flesh and blood,
As our green-mailed sons of sword and shield
From the lint-clad stranger's onset reeled,
Seeding thick the battle-field!

As, upon the growing, blowing blast,
Whistling gore drops sped like hailstones past,
Blent with hair, grey brain, and trunkless head,
Knot and clot, till filled the furrows red,
With our brave Danelanders dead!

As our Sitric sank, our Sigurd fell,
Died our Carlus and wheat-haired Conmel;
As our wounded Anrud, pierced and caught
His Erse victor, and, both struggling, sought
Hela's lake of fire and froth!

Sweet was Anrud's deed, but sweeter far
Brodar's glory, bright as Polar star!
Blest our Viking—blest his moon-cold blade!
That through Brian's brain a pathway made,
Whence emerged the Erse king's shade!

Here I heard my father's homing foot
Striking 'gainst a blasted pine tree's root;
Serious he, with eyes that seldom wept,
In whose deeps dry wrath a vigil kept—
Orbs which hardly ever slept!

They divined my deed—O son! that night,
Fell, like Winter's rain, his big tears white;
Rose, like Summer's dust, his choking curse
On the men and matrons of the Erse—
On the sons they breed and nurse!

Them might Thor's Ban-dog of Darkness gnaw;
Rend with mangling tooth and strangling claw!
Them might fiery Lok's sev'n twisted chain
Bind and blind on Hela's pitchy plain,
For our Northern Ravens slain!

"Hako," said he, " my wee blue-eyed Dane,
When you and your brothers grow amain,
When the fire of blooded manhood comes
Flaming to avenge long orphaned homes,
Read again these Saga tomes!

" Then, perchance, stirred by their mystic words,
Once again shall flash our Northern swords;
Who shall seek anew Cluain-Tarav's strand
Who will win anew the old green land,
Guided by Great Odin's hand?"

Old and cold am I, Hako, his son!
All my brothers to Nifleimir gone.
Never Norseman rose with blade and brand!
Never sighed to win the old green land!
Never sought Cluain-Tarav's strand!

In Nifleimir, too, soon shall I rot—
Song and sword and sorrow all forgot,
Who should in Valhalla live anew,
Holding silvern shield and spear of yew,
Girt with cloak of gold and blue!

Who should sit by Odin's festive board,
Sipping nectar that his bees had stored!
Vain, now, for a hero's death I sigh—
Gods! were there an Erseman near me, I
Smiting him, would happy die!

THE VISION OF ST. MALACHI O'MORGAIR

(A.D. 1148.)

"The first day's journey of a soul to pay tribute is to Jerusalem; the second to the River Jordan; the third to Adam's Paradise; the fourth, to the Royal Kingdom; the fifth to scorching Hell; the sixth to its body again; the seventh, it advances to battle."—Leabhar Breac, p. 34 B.

Break o' the Day! With a fond farewell
To the old, old home, he loved so well,
The voyager, taking scrip and stave,
Winged and shod, for vapour and wave,
Goeth—his pinions, as yet, unfree—
With golden shoon, o'er the glistering sea,
To seek a land where a cresset lights
The over skies and the under heights;
Then, reaching the rock and holy vaults
Where suffered and slept a King, he halts!

He kneels till dawn, on the memoried mount;
Then, rising, looks for a native fount,
To cleanse his eyes in its saving tide—
Light and gloom are its either side!
He finds: his chaliced palm he lowers,
Sprinkling himself with diamond showers
Of sparkling light from the river's flow,
Gemming his pate and hair and brow;
Till, on his forehead, a star is lit,
To guide him on through the Infinite!

Another dawn! Swift, adown the slopes
Of the cedar hill and olive copse,
He goes, till stayed by a garden gate,
Where, standeth one, with a sword of Hate;
But the pilgrim passes beyond the bar,
Uplifted, when seen the sacred star;
And he tastes o' the tree of golden fruit,
O' the fountain bubbling beside its root;
And he feels the airs of the flow'ry land,
Fanning his brow, like his mother's hand!

Break o' the day! Lo, a wood dove's wings
His tresses brush, and refreshed, he springs
To journey on. With his plumes released,
He soars aloft to the Great High Priest,
To azure bastions, through ruby door,
'Neath amethyst ceil, o'er golden floor,

Past youthful singers, who sweetly choir,
Past princes in white, with palm and tire;
Till, folded his wings, and bent his knees,
And drooped his head, as the Priest he sees!

Another dawn! But how dull its beam
To him, like light in a troubled dream,
As whirling down to a land of ire,
He rolls to forests and floods of fire—
Where people gasp with tongue-tortured speech,
Hoarse as the groan of a hollow beech—
Their meat of fire and their drink of flame,
Whose joys are griefs, and whose glory, shame:
The pilgrim poising above them, sees
For an hour and a day, their agonies.

Another dawn! Growing vaguely dim,
Or sun-bright—whichever holdeth him—
Hope luminous, or malign Despair—
As buoyant he floats through folds of air
To the Earth again. He cometh home
To the olden chair, the olden room;
But quenched the fire, the embers strewn,
Where darkness and shudd'ring doubt commune,
He waits and fears the slow-coming dawn—
The last, and eternal fateful one!

Break o' the day! Loud, a trumpet blows—
The fray, the fray! Forth the pilgrim goes.
Thrice blest, if girded with sword of Truth,
With helm of Hope and with shield of Ruth,
Won from his Monarch to guard his home,
To have and to hold when foemen come—
O, Victor, crowned in high glory-halls!
O, Helot, chained down 'mid shrieking thralls!—
Armed or unarmed, a soul dreadful fray
Is won or lost, on this seventh day!

Such, O my spirit! thy pilgrimage,
For full seven dawns—to Holy Ridge,
To Stream and Garden, to Heaven and Hell,
To the Earth again, till sounds a knell
Or pæan—for doom or for paradise!
Mindful of which, vague terrors rise,
Lest thou hast not won the gifts of God,
To fight and enter His bright abode;
For fierce these foemen of demon band,
Barring the way to the Promised Land!

Malachi, Son of Dermot, am I,
Who ope the Book of Eternity,
Who limn the way of each pilgrim soul—
The path to pleasure, the road to dole!

God be my luminer, and my light,
Bringing me safe to His holy sight,
Giving me falchion and cloak and shield,
For my salvation's great battle-field !
May the poor singer of this true song,
Tread the right passage, and struggle strong !

DERVORGIL AT MELLIFONT.

[NOTE.—Dervorgil, wife of Tiernan O'Rourke, Prince of
Breffni—the Irish Helen—after her elopement with Dermot
MacMurrough in 1152, retired to Mellifont Abbey, where she
died in 1193, aged 85, after a long penance of forty years.
Donal O'Melaghlin, her brother, was poisoned in 1152;
Dermot, her abductor, died of a loathsome disease in 1171;
while Tiernan, her husband, was assassinated by DeLacy in
1172.]

A flutter, then a sigh. The moon, a cloth
Wove snowy 'fore an altar, where a moth
Had gnawed at marble, where a white-haired queen
Who sought for crumbs of peace, had, sleeping, been
Enclasping flints of pain, till voice and wing
Proclaimed in each, the inward quivering sting
Of disappointment. 'Fore the shrined alcove
The dreamer knelt, on whom the face, above,
Of Mary, gracious smiled; while, in mid air,
A ruddy spark issued a current prayer.
Slow swaying, to and fro; like soul, albright,
Which moves on earth, with God's essential light,
And flames dusk wandering atoms.

Now, anear,
Came breathless footsteps, mounting tier on tier
Of winding stair, and soon, a fresh young face
Peered in and pierced the moon's wind-restless rays,
The dreamer shrouding : —

"Madam, art thou ill?"
Asked anxious lips, which did not close, but still
Awaited, as if listening nerval sense,
Affraught, had flown to them. The calm, intense,
No answer travelled; so the white-coifed nun,
Dove timid, crept anigh the sleeping one,
Dream-harried there. "O, Sainte Viérge Marie!—
Dear Madam, wake thee!" Came a dawn, slowly
Into the vacant eyes, where soon the sun
Of reason beamed, and roused a slumbering tone,
From sheeting lips :—"Is't thou, sweet Angélie?
Lo, God has touched my soul with misery,
Dreaming, that I was dead! Come, let us go,
Dear Norman!"

Then, a face, like frozen snow,
Rain-washed and shrunken grey, was pressed to hers,
Young Angélie's—whose eyes brimmed bright with
tears,
As going, she subdued her eager pace,
And matched the aged footsteps, trace for trace,
Slowly; till, reached, their oakenpanelled cell,
They heard the pealing of the turret bell.

" My dream, Angélie?—I had gone to pray
To Mary, Refuge of all Sinners; for, to-day,
My life's great crime, hid in the roll of years,
Two score—leaped out alive. My prayers and tears,
The heart's twin elements—its heat and rain,
I offered to the Mother, to obtain
From Him, her Son, the flowers of holy peace,
To soothe my life's last years. 'Mid agonies,
They came, like human blooms!

                    ⁻ I fell asleep;
For I had lingered long; when, from the deep,
Rang out a voice:—' This night, I ride alone,
Without my guards!'—Dear Angélie, my own,
Once whispered to my lover, 'fore we fled
To thorny bowers of bliss!

                  ¨Then, Dermot, dead,
Appeared before me—God, the charnel sight!
There, for his eyes, two worms gave ghastly light,
Blood red, as eclipsed moons: fast, to his ears,
With ivory teeth, like pointed, flinten spears,
Two Norway rats clung, feasting; while a host
Of green efts, from his heart crawled out, and crossed,
With grimy mouths, and points, trailing with spume,
Of ooze corrupt, breathing a deathful fume
Of sickening taint!

                'This night, I ride alone,
Without my guards!'—the horrid, crunching tone

Re-echoed through his scull ; till, frightened, swarmed
A brood of multipedes, like imps alarmed,
Thronging the gaping mouth, feelers and feet,
That miniatured the rigging of a fleet,
Twined inextricably, within a cove,
O'erridden by a whirlwind. 'Hasten, love—
Dervorgil, 'tis full time !' He touched my cheek
With gaunt and fleshless hand. I tried to shriek,
As, loosened from its socket, crumbling, fell
The joint into my bosom. With a knell,
Like quivering madness from a fire-struck bell,
My heart thrilled at its touch, and, cinering red,
It passed to ashes. Then, I withered—dead !

"I stood before my Judge !—A seraph near,
Read from a scroll, with accents, heaving fear,
Like summer's thunder :—'Lo, this woman's pride
Compassed the death of Donal !'

        ' By my side,
My guardian spirit said :—' Nine red lamps burn
Through day and dark, above his tomb and urn,
At Durrow's fane !'

       ' Again, the lector cried :—
' This wife, a husband's primal right defied,
A paramour obeying !'

                                    ˙ Said the voice:—
'For her, a convent choir, at Cluainmacnoise,
Singeth away her sin!'
                                    The seraph then,
The passage scratching with fire-pointed pen,
Exclaimed:—'This woman's virtue luring smile
Brought woe and ruin red, upon our Isle
Of Saints!'
            ˙'Replied, my pleading angel guard:—
'At Mellifont, a million folds retard
The feet of Justice—Mercy's cerement,
Woven with plaints and prayers!'
                                    Aside, I went,
Sighing, to kneel for sentence. Then, thy voice,
Angélie, called me; and, methinks, it was
The same, which pleaded for me. Sooth'd again,
Am I, of happy heart and placid brain!"

"Dear Madam," said Angélie, "at vespers,
My mind afar did go from chaunts and prayers,
Dream wand'ring. Soon, within a tangled wood
I caught my erring feet, where solitude
Reigned seemingly, till came a bleating cry
Deep from a brake, suppiercing leaf and sky,
And, from my rustling efforts, fled a horde
Of wolves, abandoning a ewe!"
                                    "Dear Lord!"
Dervorgil gasped. From off the wimpling cloth,

Her hair enfolding, flew a feasted moth,
Back, tō the altar, where a beam had sped
Midward, and clothed the swaying spark of red,
With lustrous bandle; like, when Heaven's choir
Adds to a heart's pray'r flame, a purer fire!

THE GREEN WOODS OF SLEW.

(SLIEV MARGY.)

[A lament for Rory Oge O'More, assassinated by MacGilla Patrick, June 30, 1578. Owny, mentioned in the concluding stanza, was Rory's son.]

In the heart of the forest, a thrush 'gan to sing
Of losses, the sorest—the death of a king!—
Soon, to his bough, leafless, my sympathy flew;
For I, too, roamed chiefless, in the Green Woods of
    Slew.

He, high, 'bove the heather, I, low, 'mong the fern,
Mourned sadly together—a bird and a kerne!—
Cried he, the sky winger:—"A hawking cuckoo
Has slain the chief singer of the Green Woods of
    Slew!"

Like his, was my story:—"Our glory is o'er;
For dead lies young Rory—the valiant O'More!
The scourge of the stranger, he chased the false crew,
Like a wolfhound of danger, in the Green Woods of
    Slew!

"My curse chill your castle, Gilla Patrick, the base!
No Saxon Queen's vassal, was Rory of Leix!
The Palesmen he vanquished: they parleyed with
   you;
And I am left anguished, in the Green Woods of
   Slew!

"Smile, Sidney and Perrot!—the gold, that oft
   failed—
Wise weasel, fierce ferret!—on the Gaelga prevailed:
The friend of his bosom, proved faint and untrue,
And left me heart-woesome in the Green Woods of
   Slew!"

To joy, turned our singing; for,· free from its nest,
A fledgling came winging, with many a rest:
The gold its crest tins'ling, like dawn o'er the blue—
Another plumed princeling for the Green Woods of
   Slew!

Away, sorrow blinding!—leave to women, the dead—
Far better be grinding, the grey axe, instead;
For soon, brave and bonny, from the hand of Mac
   Hugh,
Shall fly little Owny, to the Green Woods of Slew!

THE DEATH OF ART O'NEILL.

Scene : The Red Mountain (Sliabh Ruadh) over Glenmalure.
Time : Christmas, 1592.

To wild Glenmalure, o'er the snowy heights, by night
    a henchman sped—
Slow steps of pain were his, and false, on many a
    drifted bed ;
But his last, sad breath had gone to God ere he left
    his task untried,
That brought to the sons of the Ulster chiefs some
    succour, else they died !

Long the mongrel Saxon of the Pale had in chains
    these young ones held ;
But the mongrel Saxon of the Pale had not their
    spirits quelled !
Alas ! have they left a tyrant's clutch for the cold
    death-grasp of snow ?
Ah, the henchman sighed, as he thought of Hugh and
    Art, in the vale below.

" O, kind Mary, help me on and on !" he prayed, "till
    my numbed hands feel,
'Till my strained eyes see O'Byrne's hold, 'till my
    sighs to him appeal !
Lo, was that a light?   O mild Mary, sweet ! do I see
    his postern gate ?
And is that brave Feagh MacHugh himself who
    stands by the iron grate ?"

Full, many a chill qualm shook the voice, though the
    heart was warmed with ale,
And in Feagh's grave eyes of Irish grey, two
    mourners wept the tale ;
And many a big, white tear-drop welled, as his clans-
    men swept the land,
With their welcome food and warming draught in
    the welcomer, warmer hand !

How they wondered, these huge Wicklow kerns, as
    they strode with native strength—
Though they seldom marvelled at aught before—at
    the aching journey's length,
Till Sliabh Ruadh loomed above their heads, like a
    giant robed in white,
Where fast in the ice-folds at his feet lay the lost
    ones of the night !

Oh ! a bitter, burning Gaelic curse shook the rime
    on that mound of woe,
As the clansmen broke on the faces pale their
    hardened masks of snow—

Good God! have they lain in fine-threaded shirt, and
    in coat of silken gear?
Was there never a woman to pity them, all the ways
    from Dublin, here?

But these clansmen's hearts, so hard in war, are as
    soft as a maid's, in peace;
And the never a woman in Ireland's Isle could be
    half as kind as these!
But the arts of love for life are vain when the heart
    lies cold in death—
On young Art O'Neill's dumb, purple lips stayed
    frozen his dying breath!

Brave are ye, Saxons of Dublin, when ye fight with a
    swordless foe—
Sure, ye never turn the ankle round when there
    falleth no bladed blow!
But, Dar Dhia! soon your courage sinks when there
    comes an equal test
With the bristling clans of the Wicklow vales, sword
    to sword, and breast to breast!

Hugh Roe! life in you yet lingers faint—God leaves
    you to Ulster still,
Oft again you will walk in freedom o'er your heath-
    brown, breezy hill!—
With their chains' clank in your memory, with
    O'Neill tombed in your heart—
Can you ever forgive our Saxon foe, or forget young
    murdered Art?

THE TOMB OF HUGH MacCAWELL.

[Tutor of the Princes Henry and Hugh O'Neill of Tyrone, afterwards Archbishop of Armagh. Born at Saull, 1571; died at Rome, 1626.]

In your dark crypt, Isidoro,
  By the Tiber's tawny flow,
    Sleepeth one—dear Erin's son,
Whom you cherished, Isidoro,
  Long ago!

High above, on votive tablet,
  Princely Shaun, the Lord Tyrone,
    Graved the name and words of fame—
Marked them on the marble tablet,
  For his own.

"Pray for Father Hugh MacCawell,
  Of the Kinel-Fary race;
    Saull of Down, his natal town.
May the soul of Hugh MacCawell
  Rest in peace!"

Once o'er him a blade was lifted,
  That would give the accolade,
    But his lord, ere sank the sword,
High in shiny tremblance lifted,
  He gainsayed.

Praying: "Sire, withhold this honour;
  For a King of life and light
    Taketh me, and maketh me,
Poor, unworthy of such honour,
  His own knight!"

So, in place of hero-circle
  On the youth's dark curly head,
    Shone the shaven crown of heaven—
Shone St. Francis' hairless circle,
  White, instead!

Shone the crown in Aracœli,
  Far from land, and far from home:
    Shone in Spain, and in Louvain—
First, in marbly Aracœli;
  Last, in Rome!

Shone, till him the Pontiff Urban,
  Gave, with kiss of father sweet,
    Gold ring rare, and cross and chair,
Holding for the saintly Urban
  Patrick's seat.

But nor town nor Isle of Patrick
　　Soothed again his yearning eyes;
　　　　Sick he grew, one ev'ning blue,
Far from the green Isle of Patrick—
　　And its skies!

Mingling with his exile-fever
　　Burned the blood-fire of the frame;
　　　　Leech in vain, from Papal train—
Vain to cure the double fever.
　　Calming came.

Said the exile—"Lo! God calls me,
　　And He beckons me to-day:
　　　　Though it grieve you, I must leave you,
Friends, to Him my Sovereign calls me—
　　Come away!"

"Brother Emun, dearest comrade,
　　Cross and ring, my fortune, take!
　　　　You, Antoine, when I am gone,
Wear my habit, faithful comrade,
　　For my sake!"

These his latest words as gazing,
　　At a Form stretched on the Rood,
　　　　Sped the soul of Hugh MacCawell;
And his brethren, mutely gazing,
　　Understood.

Lo, we hear the voice of Urban:—
    "Not a man, indeed, was Hugh:
        But an angel—God's evangel!"
And the voice of saintly Urban
    Tearful grew.

Long for him in Isidoro
    Cheeks were pale and eyes were dim.
        Sons of Erin, wandering herein,
To his crypt in Isidoro
    Pray for him!

AWAITING OWEN ROE.

(A.D. 1642.)

Owen Roe has left the Flemings' town,
  In the lands of Nether Spain,
With many a mark, and many a crown,
  For Ireland's cause, again!
With many a bar of golden ore,
  And the Pope's red signet stone;
But we have here, a richer store
  For him, in Green Tiröen!

Móreen, my Vanithee, will place
  A rosary in his hand;
And young Nóreen will go and grace
  His breast, with ribbon band;
And my little gilla Hugh, will lead
  A steed of glossy roan;
But a kinsman's blade is my own meed
  For him, in Green Tiröen!

'Round the quigal lonely spiders weave:
   The spinet sleeps in dust;
And the caman* rots beneath the eave;
   And the plough is red with rust!
No more we spin, or sport, or toil;
   For our tyrants bold have grown,
And strangers till the weeping soil
   Of our heart lov'd Tiröen!

Oh, the rosary will win him grace:
   The breast-knot win him love;
And the steed will fly with lightning pace,
   And the sword will trusty prove!
My Móreen, pray: my Nóreen, sigh:
   Go, Hugh, and feed the roan;
For soon our swords shall sweep the sky
   For Ireland and Tiröen!

---

  * Quigal (cuigal), a distaff; caman, a crooked stick used
for hurling

THE BONNIE LIGHT HORSEMAN

(A JACOBITE BALLAD.)

A poor lonely maiden, I'm now going over
To Shemus, in Flanders, to look for my lover:
O, Mary, my pity! how shall I discover
    My bonnie light horseman, away in the war?

We lived by the banks of the broomy Blackwater,
My father and mother, and I, their one daughter,
Till red grew our valley with burning and slaughter,
    By Kirke's Saxon butchers, let loose in the war!

We fled to the cave—to the haunt of the Torie;
And Emun, my lover, for vengeance and glory,
Took sabre and steed—sad, O, Mary, my story!—
    A bonnie light horseman, he joined in the war!

I parted from him on the street of Dungannon:
He lost at the Boyne, but he won at the Shannon;
Till Shemus, the Craven, left him at Duncannon—
    My bonnie light horseman, so brave in the war!

From Limerick, with Sheldon, away he went sailing:
"Forget him, dear Eileen!" my parents cried, wailing:
They're now in the clay, while I sigh, unavailing,
    For my bonnie light horseman, afar in the war!

They've told me!—ah, love, shall I never more see
    you?
Now, Erin, cold, cold is the hand that would free
    you!—
They've told me at last—"O, asthoreen mo chree hu!"
    My bonnie light horseman is slain in the war!

THE TWO RÓSÍNS.

(A Jacobite Song.)

[As Rósin Gal (fair young Rose) the bard apostrophises his
sweetheart, and as Rósin Dhu (dark young Rose) his other
love, Ireland.]

My Rósin Gal—my Rósin Dhu,
How can I share my heart with you?
Like the sky surtinged by the morning's blush,
And the greenwood gladdened by song of thrush;
Like the home made warm by the turf fire's heat,
With a dear one throned in a rosy seat;
As a pulse by a love-look stirred and thrilled,
And the heart with the sudden rapture filled;
As a flower awaked by the sun's first kiss—
So my life by the fair young Rósin is!

O, Rósin Gal—O, Rósin Dhu,
How can I share my heart with you?
Ah! the sky is sad in the twilight pale,
With a redbreast telling a Winter tale;
And the home is cold where no hearth fires glow,
With a dear one pining in want and woe;

Ah! the throb of her pulse grows faint and weak,
And her heart can never a solace seek;
As a flower close shut, till the kiss of morn
Lies my dark Rósin, and my heart is lorn!

O, Rósin Gal—O, Rósin Dhu,
　　How must I share my heart with you?
Ah, my glad white Rose! it is bliss to me,
By thy side to sit 'neath the wild-ash tree;
For never thy heart hath a sorrow known.
And the fair wide world still is all thine own—·
A flower on a hill far from meadow bee,
Thou bloomest contented for love of me;
And the girl that trembles to bruise a blade,
Hath a path through the minstrel's bosom made!

Glad Rósin Gal—sad Rósin Dhu,
　　How must I share my heart with you?
Ah! my sad red Rose, hath a ruthless band
Thy warm heart crushed on the arid sand?
Doth an upas keep the pure light away
With its poisonous odour of decay?
Do drones sip thy nectar, still fresh and sweet,
And profane thy leaves with their guilty feet?
Must my brothers and I shake cruel gyves,
And passing not raise thee to save our lives?

Still, Rósin Gal—still, Rósin Dhu,
Thus I can share my heart with you!
Thou, my fair white Rose, take its cherished Love,
Faithful till summoned with thee above!
Sweet maid, thou hast won it fair of me
Beneath the ripe beads of the quicken tree!—
Thou, my sad red Rose, take its life, if so,
It lays at thy feet a detested foe!
Then quickly command, that I may behold,
A glad red Rose bloom as in days of old!

D

THE LITTLE HARVEST ROSE.

(A.D. 1745.)

There's a ripple on the waters of our four wide seas;
  There's a murmur on the mountains, like at dawning hour;
There's a whisper 'mong the ash trees, as they shake their keys,
  And a thrill stirs all the sleeping land with wond'rous power.
For, the sowing time is coming, with its lingering days,
  When the fields no longer slumber 'neath the winter snows,
When we'll plant the Tree of Liberty, 'mid hymns of praise,
  And greet, again, our long-lost, little Harvest Rose!

'Mong the glens of Kinel Fary, in the land of Owen,
  We await the morning whistle of The Blackbird, clear:
From the royal heights of Aileach, to the Golden Stone,
  We are ready, all—kerne, gallowglass, and mountaineer.

Soon, we'll plough the fields with horses' hoof and
  soldiers' foot;
    And we'll water them, till fetlock high, the black
      blood flows;
Then, we'll plant the Tree of Liberty, of spreading
  root,
    And greet again our little, shining, Harvest Rose!

Long, our little, shining, Harvest Rose has blighted
  been
    By the cruel, clinging, Red Wind from the charnel
      East—
Every branch and bloom lay stricken, till no leaf of
  green
    Could greet the hopeful, longing eyes of chief
      or priest!
Still, we're watching and we're waiting, for the pass of
  night,
    Till the saffron dawn wind o'er the hills of glory,
      blows,
That will bear a morning summons on its wings of
  light,
    For the budding of our little, shining, Harvest
      Rose!

Hark, a clarion is resounding from the Grampian
  Hills—
    'Tis the whistle of The Blackbird, at the dawn of
      day!

Every heart with rosy rapture, at the songburst
    thrills,
  As we rise from rushy bed and bush to join the
    fray.
As we go, our daughters speed our path, with praise
    and prayer,
  And a blush on every mantling cheek, like sunset,
    glows;
But a redder, sweeter blossom, we will welcome, fair,
  When we greet again, our little, shining, Harvest
    Rose!

Translations from the Gaelic.

MARY MAGUIRE.
(Turlough Carolan.)*

'Tis my tear and sigh, that my dear and I
　Woo not 'mid the pleasant highlands,
With never a tone, but our own, alone,
　To break the slumbering silence!

But—O King of Grace!—what need to praise
　My gentle sweetheart, blushing,
For love of whom, sharp arrows come
　All through my body rushing?

At the early dawn she goes o'er the bawn,
　With her twisted coolun gleaming;
And her bright face glows like a white wild rose,
　Through the sunlit dewdrops beaming!

---

* For the original see Hardiman, Vol. II., page 8.

O, her soft skin, smooth !—O, her honey mouth,
Harp sweet, that never wearies !
Swan's neck of snow, and cheeks where grow
Two ruddy rowan berries !

THE BROWN THORN.

(From the Gaelic.*)

Oh, many a one that came to woo believed my heart
    was all his own,
But when he spoke of love to me I heard anew my
    lover's tone:
And so my suitors swiftly passed down Slieve
    O'Flinn, like driven snow—
For the sake of him, as fair and white, as the spiky
    blossoms of the sloe.

O love! O love! what woe is mine this day, to think
    'twas gold you sought;
That I am left alone in grief, because no hoarded
    wealth I brought!
O ruthless one! who pained my heart—in vain, this
    night, I pant and pray,
That we may meet, when white's the dew, in a
    mountain valley far away!

---

* For the original, see Miss Brooke's *Reliques of Irish
Poetry*, page 306.

Here, in my purse, deep down and close, I hold a
keepsake of my love;

But all the men in Innisfail my load of sorrow could
not move!

When thoughts of him rush through my mind—O
hero of the tresses brown—

The live long day, the dead long night, my tears in
silence trickle down.

A present from my brown-haired boy would cure my
grief the next Fair day;

Or greeting kind and winning smile from the flower
of youth upon the way—

Oh, would to God! a priest were near, to calm my
bitter biting woe,

By joining my fond love to me, before across the
seas he go!

Oh, should he not think bad of me, my lips will
praise him, far and wide;

And should he not think bad of me, I shall seat my-
self close by his side;

And should he not think bad of me, my eyes will
wound with many a dart —

O Star of Light!—before the world, I hide my own
poor bleeding heart!

O God above, what shall I do, if he should turn his
back on me?—

For all unknown to me his house — unknown his
hearth and family.

My mother moves with many a sigh, my father
    stumbles all the day,

And angry are my kith and kin—and he, my darling,
    far away!

A cloud of woe enfolds my eyes, and sleep comes
    never brushing near—

I think of him, my first lost love, and every night
    seems as a year:

Mocked by the world for loving him, who loves me
    not—whose heart is cold!

Alas, Sweet Branch! why did you come—why have
    you me a falsehood told?

GRACE NUGENT.

(From the Gaelic of Turlough O'Carolan.*)

No trouble 'tis for me to praise my whitest flower of
    fairness,
  My Gracie Og, the sweetest of all maids that be:
Who bears the palm for excellence, for beauty, and
    for rareness,
  From all the Fair and Fragrant of the whole
    countrie!

Who ever can you find me, who has lingered in her
    presence,
  Could say there came one moment's thought of ill
    for him?
Queen of the gentle graces and the winning ways of
    pleasaunce,
  Of the free branching tresses and the ringlets prim!

---

* For the original, see **Walker's** *Historical Memoirs of the
Irish Bards*, page 76.

Like lime her skin, like swan her neck, white arching
   'bove each shoulder—
The sun of summer is her face at dawning clear.
O blessèd fortune for him who will woo and win and
   hold her—
   Sweet branch of tendrils curling thick the live-long
   year!

Oh, very choice, to heart and ear, her silvery con-
   versation;
And very bright and beautiful her eyes of blue;
I hear the praises sounding everywhere throughout
   the nation
Of her wavy tresses wandering from neck to shoe.

I say, and say it o'er again, sweet maid, more true
   your singing
   Than all the birds on all the trees, on all the
   plains—
No balm that ever heart desired to soothe a sorrow
   wringing,
   But may be found—my hand on it—in Gracie's
   strains!

Her teeth in rows unbroken, and her hair in ringlets
   shining—
Ochón! 'tis late, my pleasant task I must leave so;
Yet from a heart that, many a time, for Gracie has
   been pining,
   I'll drink my darling's health, once more, before I
   go!

SHOHEEN SHO.*

[A woman was once taken by the fairies through one of them assuming the voice of her husband, and thus enticing her into their lios. Here she remained seven years, nursing the children of the fairies. One day, while rocking a fairy child at the lios door, she saw a woman washing clothes down at the river, whom she thus importuned for help :—]

O woman! down, at the flag-stones, cleaning,
Take pity, now, on my bitter keening:

To her fairy nurse child :—

Shoheen sho!—ulla lo!—
Shoheen sho! thou'rt not my darling!

'Tis seven years since a fairy, cruel,
Enticed me hither, to meet my jewel!
Shoheen sho! etc.

---

* For the Gaelic original, see John O'Daly's *Miscellany*, page 109. Another version of this song has been beautifully rendered by Dr. Sigerson.

Since then, the babes of a dozen fairies,
I've nursed for them, till my bosom wearies!
    Shoheen sho! etc.

Oh, help me, woman! and homewards, going,
Put down a fire, wide tongued and glowing.
    Shoheen sho! etc.

Seize, then, the old hag, white-haired, and faded,
That seven years hath my bed invaded!
    Shoheen sho! etc.

Upon her back, in the broad blaze, heave her—
Let the whole world see the foul deceiver!
    Shoheen sho! etc.

Tell, then, my husband to rise and dress him;
And seek the priest, who will solemn bless him.
    Shoheen sho! etc.

A knife, black helved, in his right hand, holden,
Let him reach this lios, by the dawning golden!
    Shoheen sho! etc.

And cut three stalks by the door shaft, shaded—
Two, fine stemmed, and one broad-bladed.
    Shoheen sho! etc.

These be our daughters and son, brown curled,
Transformed at the door of the fairies' world!
    Shoheen sho! etc.

For oh! fay child, whom I rock, heart-woesome,
For thee, no true love can warm my bosom!
    Shoheen sho!—ulla!—lo!—
    Shoheen sho!—thou'rt not my darling!

THE CLAY OF THE CHURCH OF CREGGAN.

(From the Irish.*)

THE BARD:

Near the clay of Creggan's churchyard I lay last
    night in grief,

But with the dawn a maiden's kiss brought my poor
    heart relief;

Her cheeks glowed like twin roses red, her hair like
    purest gold—

'Twas the greatest pleasure of my life this princess to
    behold!

THE FAIRY:

Free-hearted, friendly mortal, cast all sorrow to the
    wind:

Arise, and Westland come with me, and happiness
    thou'lt find

Far in the Land of Promise, where never a stranger
    trod—

Come to its music-palaces and leave this lonely sod!

---

* For the original, see Nicholas Kearney's *Transactions of
the Ossianic Society*, Vol. II.

THE BARD:

O, princess sweet! who art thou? The young Helen,
    bright as sun?
Or from the rare Parnassian Nine art thou a chosen
    one?
What country in the world wide hath reared thee,
    cloudless star,
Who seek'st an humble minstrel bard for a love
    whisperer?

THE FAIRY:

Oh! ask not, for I live not at this side south of the
    Boyne,
A child from Grenogue's borders, for love's tenderness
    I pine:
Oft in the bardic houses have I waked the *clair-
    seach's** tone,
At evening in Temora† and at morning in Tyrone.

THE BARD:

I would not spurn thy love, sweet one, for all the
    wealth of kings;
Yet must I leave all friendship now, and all the joy it
    brings:
The sweetheart whom I flattered with my promises
    of old—
Oh, must I leave her desolate, and never her face
    behold?

---

* *Clairseach*, a small harp used by minstrels. † Temora, Tara.

THE FAIRY:

Methinks thou'rt friendless, spite of all thy kindred
    dear and near;

I see thee garmentless and poor, a despised wanderer;

And better for thee dwell with me, gold-curled and
    young and white,

Than have the Saxons mocking the harsh-rhyming
    doggrel wight!

THE BARD:

Yea, 'tis my bitter sorrow that the Tyrowen Gaels
    are dead,

And that the chieftains of the Fews are long since
    banishèd—

The green shoots of Neill Frasach, the great music-
    loving band,

Who gave me food and raiment when cold winter
    chilled the land.

THE FAIRY:

These tribes at Aughrim have been crushed, and at
    the bloody Boyne,

Brave Miledh's heirs, who learning loved, who
    sheltered friends of thine:

Then better in the *liosses** dwell with me, a fairy
    bride,

There William's† darts and vengeances we laughing
    can deride!

---

* The fairy forts or raths.   † William III.

THE BARD:

O, princess sweet, it is my fate! My treasure, I will
    go;
But give thy promise that when I in death shall
    stretch me low,
By Shannon's side, on Manan's Isle, or e'en in Ægypt
    great,
Thou'lt lay my corse in Creggan's clay, and I will
    feel elate:

THE DARK MAIDEN OF THE VALLEY.*

(Bean Dubh an Gleanna.)

Oh, have you seen, or have you heard, my treasure
of bright faces,

    Some dark glen roving, while in gloom I pine here
day and night?

Far from her voice, far from her eyes, my cloud of
woe increases—

    My blessing on that glen and her, for aye and aye
alight.

'Tis many's the time they've put in print, to beauty
doing homage,

    Her figure tall, her eyebrows small, her thin-lipped
mouth of truth,

Her snowy hands, as fair and fine as silk or wild
bird's plumage—

    My bitter sigh to think that I am here, a lonely
youth !

---

* The title is somewhat misleading, and really is " The
Maiden of the Dark Valley." For the original, see Miss
Brooke's *Reliques*, page 319.

One little glance, once at her face, a flame lit in my
    bosom,

    O, snowy-breasted, white-toothed one, whose ring-
        lets are of gold,

More dear art thou than Deirdré, leaving lovers
    mourning woesome,

Or Blanaid, meshing thousands with her winning
    eyes of old!

O, bloom of women! spurn me not for this rich
    suitor hoary—

    This boorish, noisy, songless man, who comes
        between us twain;

It's I would sweetly sing beneath the harvest moon's
    gold glory,

    For thee full many a Fenian lay and bold Milesian
        strain!

GUGGIE O'GAIG.

[A dialogue between an old goose and a gosling, para-
phrased from the Gaelic in John O'Daly's *Miscellany*,
page 111.]

I.

GOSLING.

Say where, Mother Guggie, shall I make my nest?
When far from the warmth of thy comforting breast?

GOOSE.

White wrapped in the bed,
Go nestle thy head,
O, tired little bird by no fond one caressed—
My poor Guggie O'Gaig a-seeking a nest!

GOSLING.

But, mother, the nurse
Would come with a curse,
All hoarsely and coarsely in anger expressed!—
Say where, Mother Guggie, shall I make my nest?

II.

GOOSE.

The cradle go sleep in,
Where no one will peep in,
To creep in or leap in, to break on the rest
Of my Guggie O'Gaig, there making her nest!

GOSLING.

But mother, the baby,
The wee Sheela, maybe,
Would there deeply sleep and would scream at her
    guest!—
Say where, Mother Guggie, shall I make a nest?

III.

GOOSE.

Perched proud 'neath the transome
Thou'd look mighty handsome
Securely, demurely there pluming the crest
Of Guggie O'Gaig in her cute little nest.

GOSLING.

But, mother, the colleen,
The flax-headed Molleen,
There tucks in the ducklings when red is the West!—
Say where, Mother Guggie, shall I make my nest?

IV.

GOOSE.

Perhaps in the barn
Filled golden with corn,
With neat sheaves of wheat newly girdled and pressed
My poor Guggie O'Gaig may chance on a nest.

GOSLING.

There, mother, the crashing
Of Rory when threshing
I'd hear, and I'd fear in my nook of unrest:
Say where, Mother Guggie, shall I make my nest?

V.

GOOSE.

Go down to the river
Where long rushes quiver,
There diving and thriving live blithely and blest,
My Guggie O'Gaig, in a sedgy-green nest.

GOSLING.

There, mother, comes gaily
A fisherman daily
To dangle and angle with patience and zest:
Say where, Mother Guggie, shall I make a nest?

VI.

GOOSE.

Fly off to the floe
In the peat bogs below,
Where flossy flake mossy, and soft as my breast,
My Guggie O'Gaig may find for a nest.

GOSLING.

There, mother, an urchin
Stays plaiting and lurching,
While minding the kine he would surely molest:
Say where, Mother Guggie, shall I make a nest?

VII.

GOOSE.

Then hie to the hill,
To the wood dense and still,
'Neath the ooze of the Spruce, where no dangers infest,
My Guggie O'Gaig, and seek for a nest.

GOSLING.

There, mother, a hunter
With shot gun and pointer
Goes fowling and prowling on many a quest.
Say where, Mother Guggie, shall I make my nest?

VIII.

GOOSE.

Maybe, on the meadows,
'Neath sun twinkling shadows
Of bog lint and marsh mint and clover white-tressed,
My Guggie O'Gaig may weave her a nest.

GOSLING.

There, mother, some morning,
Without word or warning,
A mower will lower the grass at his best.
Say where, Mother Guggie, shall I make my nest?

IX.

GOOSE.

Maybe on the moor,
Alone and secure,
Unwhirled by the world in a hollow unguessed,
My Guggie O'Gaig can build her a nest.

GOSLING.

There, mother, the plover
Around me would hover,
Low flying and crying, disturbed and distressed.
Say where, Mother Guggie, shall I make my nest?

GOOSE.

I know not, poor gosling, where safe thou can'st rest
When far from the warmth of thine own mother's
  breast!

NELLY OF BALLINTLEA.

[From the Gaelic, taken down phonetically by Mr. John McCall, from an old woman named Costello, a native of Mayo, in the year 1840.]

For the original, see *Dublin Journal of Temperance, Science, and Literature*, Vol. II., page 374.

Of a summer's morning, I once was wand'ring by the
King's highway,
Gazing enraptured on the pleasant courtyard of Bal-
lintlea;
When who tripped gaily, but little Nelly, with eyes
of grey,
Who blushed to see me, as I gave freely the time of
day.

Her brow was whiter, of lustre brighter, than of the
swan,
Or the flakes of snow, which the bleak winds blow
along the lawn;
Her flowing tresses, like golden flashes of sunbeams,
shone;
And her neck and bosom, like blackb'ry blossom, lit
by the dawn!

Again, I met her—I well remember—at the thronging
    wake:

There, no one knew me, as I roved through them, my
    place to take.

A stool, they gave me, a curious stranger, for kind-
    ness' sake,

Beside young Nelly—and who could blame me, love
    thus to make?

Deeply she listened, sweetly I whispered, how sore
    my heart

To taste her kisses and twist her ringlets, some nook
    apart;

Though many wooed her that eve, enduring a bitter
    dart,

I gained her favour—my fair betrayer, this morn,
    thou art!

Last Wednesday morning, at early dawning, madly I
    rose—

Laved not my temples, combed not my tresses, donned
    not my clothes;

But rushing wildly, where, bubbling whitely, the river
    flows,

I edged my skeean on the red clucheen, to ease my
    woes!

Fierce grew my passion, for desolation swept o'er my
    mind;

And overwhelmed me with woe and trembling and
    anger blind!—

To learn that Nelly had wed already—O, love, un-
kind !—

My arm I shattered, gashed from its socket, such
faith to find !

Ah, Nelly, darling !—why did you charm me, then
crush my love ?

Oh, could you see me, this lurid evening, and cruel
prove !

Soon, on my coffin, the woodman sawing, will work,
above ;

And comrades bear me to the gloomy graveyard, by
Killeen's grove !

Yet, were I dying, forsaken, lying stretched on my
bed,

For se'ndays seven, or till a twelvemonth had o'er me
sped,

My Nelly's kisses, her merry whispers to me, half
dead,

Afar would banish my mist of anguish from heart and
head !

KATHLEEN TYRREL.

[The author of the following little song is unknown, but the subject of it lived near Tyrrel's Pass. Lough Erril is another name for Lough Ennel. See Hardiman, page 247.]

'Tis my mood to give praise to the good and the true,
So 'tis meet I should treat of Kathleen of the Curls;
For right gracious and pleasant, bright blossom, are you,
And your like is not known 'mong the Northern girls!
'Tis my morning sigh, daily, that I did not stay,
Still to stray by the brink of Lough Erril, at dawn,
To stroll and behold your soft tresses of gold,
In beauty unrolled to each wondering one!

'Tis my grief that I ever saw pen or inkhorn,
Or the corn clustering knot of your coolun bawn, tight!—
Could our Lord Bishop raise his hand o'er us, in grace,
I would take you, far ways, o'er the salt seas to night.

You're more white than the swan, you're more bright
    than the sun;
    And more choice is your voice, than all music can
        boast—
Not an inn can be found in the town and around,
    That does not resound with your true lover's toast!

'Tis a pity, I stay not with Kitty, this day,
    'Neath the knoll of the holly—my glass to her lip—
With God's help, I would try to entice her away,
    From her mother, with me o'er the mountain to
        trip!
I have spelled her dear lines held against the drear
    . wind—
    Oh, no song from the fairies, more sweet could be
        writ—
It has swollen my heart, it has stolen my mind;
    And your soul, Kathleen Tyrrel, must answer for it!

Humorous and Characteristic Sketches.

TATTHER JACK WELSH

(A New Version.)

Did you meet e'er a boy on the road to the fair,
With his merry blue eyes and his curly brown hair,
With his hands in his pockets, and whistling a jig,
To humour the way for himself and his pig?

Oh, that was the boy who has won my fond heart,
Whose eyes have sent through me a dangerous dart;
And cut out my sweetheart of old, Darby Kelsh—
Oh, my blessing attend you, my Tatther Jack Welsh!

Well, he lives up the lane, by the side of Lug Dhu,
And the dickonce a ha'porth in life does he do,
But breaking the hearts of the girls all around—
Not a single one, whole and entire, can be found.

For he is the boy that can lilt up a tune —
Troth, you'd think 'twas the fairies were singing Da
    Luan !
Oh I your feet would go jigging in spite of yourself,
If you heard the fife played by that musical elf.

One fine evening young Darby came up to our house,
And, indeed, the poor boy was as mute as a mouse,
'Till my Jacky came in, and says he, " Darby Kelsh,
Shure you can't coort at all—look at Tatther Jack
    Welsh !"

So up the rogue rushes, and gave me a pogue* ;
And Darby ran out, like he'd got a poltogue†—
"Arrah, what can be ailing," says he, "Darby Kelsh ?"
" Haith you know well enough," says I, " Tatther
    Jack Welsh !"

---

* *Póg*, a kiss.   † *Buailtóg*, a slight beating, or crack.

OVER THE HILLS TO MARY.

(Air—"Nancy Wants her Own Share.")

The oats are down, the praties sown,
The meadows fine and green have grown,
And now my cótamore I've thrown
    Across my shoulders airy;
Just o'er the low half door I lean
And think where I will go this e'en—
When goes a thought to my young queen,
    Over the hills to Mary!

Refrain:

Yes, o'er the hills and o'er the rills,
O'er dikes and ditches, drains and drills,
But Love the way with flowers fills,
    Over the hills to Mary.

There's a dance at Pedhar Poor's to-night,
With fun *go leór* and music bright,
With maidens fair and bouchals light,
    And our fiddler, Phil O'Leary.

To Jem the Gow a paper came,
They'll read it by his forge's flame—
Yet, still I'll ramble all the same
    Over the hills to Mary!

                 Refrain.

And Mogue beyond has bought a horse,
And asked me over there, of course,
To see if I would not endorse
    His bargain, purchased chary;
While Jer and Joe and Shamus Roe
Are playing "spoil five" down below—
They're cheaters all, so off I'll go
    Over the hills to Mary!

                 Refrain.

My new wool hat I've brushed quite clean,
My bodycoat's a bottle green,
My waistcoat of a brighter sheen
    Than that of Father Cleary.
A botheen* in my fist I'll hold
To beat the dogs and ganders bold—
There's no evading them, I'm told,
    Over the hills to Mary!

                 Refrain.

---

* *Botheen,* a cudgel; *cótamore,* an overcoat; *go leór* in
abundance; *bouchals,* youths.

Just up the boreen soft I'll creep,
And o'er the haggard stile I'll leap,
And through the holly hedge I'll peep
     Right opposite the dairy;
There, 'neath her Roseen, sitting low,
She'll milk her favourite Kerry cow—
I'll whisper "Cushla!" sweet and slow
     Over the hills to Mary!

                              Refrain.

Then, when the milk-pail in I've brought,
I'll get a kiss—when her I've caught—
Now, Pat, my boy, 'tis time you ought
     To win this little fairy!
While by the fire her mother knits,
Just see if something shiny fits—
I'm off, nor longer rack my wits,
     Over the hills to Mary!

              Refrain :
Yes, o'er the hills and o'er the rills,
O'er dikes and ditches, drains, and drills,
But Love the way with flowers fills,
     Over the hills to Mary!

THRESHING THE BARLEY.

(Air—" The Cuckoo's Nest.")

[*Scene:*—The barn of a Wexford farmhouse. Pat and Mat Murphy, two brothers, are engaged threshing; seated on a bench of sheaves at the end of the barn are three companions, who have been overtaken by a shower of rain, and have come hither for shelter.]

PAT, *solus :* —

Oh, the haggard stand we've emptied, and the sheaves
    we've carried in,
And the corner of the barn to the thatch is piled
    within,
As young Mat and I, right opposite, our flails lift in
    the air;
For there's money due, and prices, too, are holdin'
    purty fair.

Chorus (by all) : —

With a crack from Pat, a smack from Mat,
    The grains like birdlings fly!
With a whack from Pat, a thwack from Mat,
    The *bólteens* quickly ply!
Oh, a pound a bar'l they're sure to get in Wexford,
    bye-an'-bye;
For there's ne'er a man in Bargy better barley can
    supply!

MAT, *solus :* —

Sure, last year, the rainy weather put our noses out
o' joint;

For the wind kept, every mornin', blowin' from the
rainy point;

And the hay was bad—the corn, bedad, was nothiu'
else but straw—

We'll make up for that, or know for what, when
this to town we draw!

Chorus : —

With a crack from Pat, etc.

PAT : —

Thank God, the sun so constant shone all through the
harvest days,

And, the pratie-diggin' keepin' dry, we picked them
at our aise.

Now the big goold champions split their sides with
laughin' in the pot,

So come, welt away till noon, and we will have them,
smokin' hot!

Chorus : —

With a crack from Pat, etc.

MAT : —

Ould Sharpes, the agent, liked our beans, and bought
them for the horse;

He settled for them on the nail—that paid the rent,
of course!

Egonneys, as he gave the change—some fifty shillin's
  o'er—
"'Tis ye that keep that same place cheap!" says he
  so sour and sore!

Chorus :—

With a crack from Pat, etc.

PAT :—

Ah, we wouldn't care a *thraneen,* only mother died
  last Shroft,
For she loved her two big gorsoons with affection
  kind and soft;
And she said when dyin':—"Mat an' Pat, let
  nothin' ever part
Ye two, an' God be with you, with the blessin' o' me
  heart!"

Chorus :—

With a crack from Pat, etc.

MAT :—

And, we'll do her biddin', Pat and I, though Pat has
  tuk, of late,
To coortin' Molly Slevin—at such work he can't be
  bate;
And, as she lives but there beyant, and she's to get
  the place,
When Mogue, the father, cocks his toes—why, Pat,
  don't hide your face!

Chorus :—

With a crack from Pat, etc.

PAT :—

Haith, true for you, you're guilty, too! well, sure,
   there's no harm done

If Kitty Larkin takes a likin' to your father's son!

Though I must admit that you could get a nicer girl
   than she—

Well, we'll lave it so!—don't angry grow, if now we
   can't agree!

Chorus :—
   With a crack from Pat, etc.

MAT :—

But, whisht! there's someone comin'—with the noise
   I couldn't hear;

Och, 'tis Nelly, and she's sayin' how the dinner time
   is near;

So, hang up your flail, and I'll go bail we'll relish and
   enjoy

A bit o' bacon, rowled in greens, and praties—Pat,
   me boy!

Chorus (by all leaving) :—

With a crack from Pat, a smack from Mat,
   The grains like birdlings fly!

With a whack from Pat, a thwack from Mat,
   The bolteens quickly ply!

Oh, a pound a bar'l they're sure to get in Wexford
   bye-an'-bye;

For there's ne'er a man in Bargy better barley can
   supply!

AN IRISH BOUCHALEEN.*

(Air—"Blackberry Blossoms.")

Oh, the jewel of my bosom is my Irish bouchaleen!

He can dig a spit, or thresh a bit—no better shure
is seen;

Aye, or dance a jig, or drive a pig, or make love to
a queen—

Oh, the darling of the world is he — my Irish
bouchaleen!

Oh, to see him in the Springtime with his horses well
in hand,

As he guides the cleaving ploughshare through the
oaten stubble land,

While his furrows as the ruling in our copies are as
straight,

And he lilts his song, "The Colleen Donn," till all is
made "complate."

---

* *Bouchaleen,* a farmer's boy.

Then with the harrow up and down, the *prashagh**
   weeds are rooted out,
   The seed is nicely scattered in the finely-powdered
      clay ;
Then, when the roller runs o'er all, and every place is
   smoothed out,
   He goes to Jem the Smith's to hear what all the
      papers say.

Chorus :—

Oh, the jewel of my bosom is my Irish bouchaleen !

He can dig a spit, or thresh a bit—no better shure
   is seen ;

Aye, or dance a jig, or drive a pig, or make love to a
   queen ;

Oh, the darling of the world is he — my Irish
   bouchaleen !

Then to see him in the Summer, how his pitchfork
   he can wield,

As he tosses up the new-mown hay, with Nelly, in the
   field ;

Or upon the rick perched cosy he puts on the wheaten
   thatch ;

Or with gun in hand, the *preecauns*† from the oats he
   has to watch.

---

* *Prashagh*, brassy-coloured flowers (ragweed, etc.).
† *Preecauns*, crows.

Aye, or mending, down the *bóreen*, the old gate, to
keep the heifer out;
Or cutting faggots on the ditch, or by the river's
brim;
Or down the bogs, a-making turf, to last the Wint'ry
weather out—
Oh, none on earth, for work or mirth, can yet com-
pare with him!

Chorus : —Oh, the jewel of my bosom, &c.

Oh, to see him in the Autumn, in the yellow harvest
time,
Is to see him in his element, his glory, and his
prime,
With his honest face above the corn, he works the
gleaming scythe,
While his laugh and smile around beguile the binders
far and wide.
Oh, he keeps them all perspiring as he cuts so fast
the nodding corn,
Till Nelly cries: "Why, Pat, agra, you're workin'
.like a horse!"
And he replies with ringing laugh, nor stops the
motion in his scorn—
"What matter, Nelly *bán astór* —I'll never be the
worse!"

Chorus : —Oh, the jewel of my bosom, &c.

But to see him in the Winter is to see the house's
    pride,

When he has the "praties" pitted and the haggard
    full outside,

Then the days are spent in threshing, and the even-
    ings all in fun—

Oh, 'tis then his loving parents know the value of
    their son!

Shure at Brian Darcy's wedding, it was he that acted
    "best man" there,

    At Kitty Cormack's christ'ning, too, he stood for
    little Shaun,

There, when we'd danced "The Kerry Jig," and
    seated by me on the chair,

    With arm around me, whispered he:—"*Acushla*,
    give me *one?*"

Chorus:—Oh, the jewel of my bosom, &c.

OLD PEDHAR CARTHY FROM CLONMORE.

If you searched the county o' Carlow, ay, and back
again,
    Wicklow too, and Wexford, for that matter you
    might try,
Never the equal of Old Pedhar would you crack
again'—
    Never such another would delight your Irish eye!
Mirth, mime, and mystery, all were close combined in
him,
    Divelment and drollery right to the very core,
As many tricks and turns as a two-year-old you'd find
in him,
    In Old Pedhar Carthy from Clonmore!
        Old Pedhar, Old Pedhar, Old Pedhar Carthy,
            Old Pedhar Carthy from Clonmore!

Shure whene'er the *bouchals* used to have a game o'
"Forty-five,"
    Pedhar was the master who could teach them how
    to play;

Bring a half-crown, though you lost it, yet, as I'm
  alive
  You'd be a famous player to your distant dying
  day.
Scornful grew his look if they chanced to hang your
  king or queen;
  Better for your peace o' mind you never crossed
  his door:
"You to play cards!" would he mutter in sarcasm
  keen—
  Old Pedhar Carthy from Clonmore!
    Old Pedhar, Old Pedhar, Old Pedhar Carthy,
    Old Pedhar Carthy from Clonmore!

Politics he knew better than the men in Parliament,
  And the wars in Europe for the past half century;
If you were to hear him with Cornelius Keogh in
  argument,
  Arranging every matter that was wrong in history!
Ah! but if the talking ever travelled back to "Ninety-
  eight,"
  Then our Pedhar's diatribes grew vehement and
  sore—
Rebel in his heart, how he hated to have long to
  wait—
  Old Pedhar Carthy from Clonmore!
    Old Pedhar, Old Pedhar, Old Pedhar Carthy,
    Old Pedhar Carthy from Clonmore!

The mischief for tricks, he was never done inventing
them;
 Once he yoked Dan Donohoe's best milker to the
plough—
At the Fair of Hacketstown there was no circum-
venting him.
 He'd clear a crowd of *salachs** and you never
could tell how!
The Ryans and the Briens and their factions were
afraid of him;
 For Pedhar's fighting kippeen could command a
ready score—
Woe to the boys that spoke *cruked*, undismayed of
him,
 Of Old Pedhar Carthy from Clonmore!
 Old Pedhar, Old Pedhar, Old Pedhar Carthy,
  Old Pedhar Carthy from Clonmore!

But the times grew bad, and the people talked so
well and wise,
 Fighting left poor Ireland, and mad mischief had
its head;
Pedhar, left alone, began to muse, and to soliloquise,
 Until the dear old fellow couldn't bear to leave the
bed;
But when dead and buried all the neighbours felt his
bitter loss—
 The place in Pedhar's absence such a look of sorrow
wore,

---

* Untidy people, tinkers, etc.

They sighed and cried in turn from great Eagle Hill
 to Cameross,
 For Old Pedhar Carthy from Clonmore!
  Old Pedhar, Old Pedhar, Old Pedhar Carthy,
   Old Pedhar Carthy from Clonmore!

  Old Pedhar, Old Pedhar, Old Pedhar Carthy,
   Old Pedhar Carthy from Clonmore!

THE MUMMERS OF BARGY.

Air—"Droghedy's March" (The Druid's Dance).

Down at the big manor-house of Kilquaun
  Assemble the girls and the boys all of Bargy—
Wondr'ous this night in the barn and the bawn
  To hear Billeen Ceól* with his pipes sweetly
    "arguy"!
      Aiden Roche, the Mummer leader,
      Came with a boy o' the Neils from Sleedhair:
      Dick Shones Phoor† is George the Valiant,
      Charley Hayes, St. Patrick gallant—
Oh, such a crowd of the girls is collected,
'Twill be a surprise if there's no one neglected!
They line all the walls like a headland of lilies,
Or rosies, or posies, or daffy-down-dillies!

The centre is clear, and the candles alight,
  When lo, from the haggard there comes a loud
    knocking;

---

* Little Billy of the Music.   † Dick, the son of John Power.

Soon quickly troop in twelve Mummers in white,
  With feathers high flying, like wild geese a-flocking.
      Round they go, two circles forming,
      Billeen the " Soldier's Joy," performing.
    - Heels keep cracking, clubs a-crashing,
      Arms a-swinging, eyes a-flashing.
In and out, round about, back to their places,
Fencing and foiling, the crowd interlaces;
Now all uncoil and in single file canter,
Yet striking and timing to Billeen's old chanter.

The war dance of " Droghedy's March " fast they play;
  Then the quick, single jig, " Nance Wants Her
      Answer,"
"The Geese in the Bog," and the grand " First o' May,"
  " The Flowers," and a Reel, for their favourite
      dancer;
      Then the Mummer's play commences,
      When St. George so bold advances,
      Tells of " draggins, elves, and jyants "
      He has killed, and hurls defiance;
Till our Saint Patrick, with green on his bonnet,
Appears on the scene, when his glove is thrown on it.
Oh! the saints fight, spite of their holy station,
And Patrick upholds the fair fame of his nation.

In comes a *dochtor*, " so pure and so good,"
  To heal the deep wounds of the saintly contender,

G

Twenty gold guineas he wants to stop blood,
 Saint Pat is *charoosed* * with the quacky pretender.
  Cromwell stalks, with nose of scarlet,
  He calls Cæsar great a varlet;
  Dan O'Connell greets Napoleon—
  E'en a *poocha* here has stolen.
Everyone, as he comes, " spachifies " neatly,
And shows off his skill and his prowess completely;
But they all make it up, just as it ought to be,
And, joining their hands in a ring, they dance
 "Droghedy."

But as this night is the last of such fun—
 Twelfth Day is nigh, and the days getting light-
  some—
So the grand *rinka* of all is begun,
 And for it the *cailins* dress beauteous and bright-
  some.
  Aiden Roche takes Alley Kelly,
  Dick Shones Phoor, Johanna Skelly,
  Charley, Anty, Mogue, young Sheela,
  Thus they mingle, *three-na-cheela*.†
Heel and toe, off they go, tripping and skipping,
Till daylight right over their shoulders is peeping.
The girls all make home at the top o' the morning,
But talk for a year of it, milking or churning!

---

 * *Charoosed*, perplexed.   † Up and down.

THE LITTLE HEATHY HILL.

(An Cnóicin Fraoic.)

AN IRISH GIRL'S STORY.

Oh, my Cauthaleen, just listen! try and stay a weenie
  while,
  Till you hear the heap of trouble that's upon me:
Sure, you know young Brian Kinsella, beyond the
  hills in Kyle,
  Cauthaleen! I fear that roguish lad has won me!
You were with me that fine day on the little heathy
  hill,
  We went *fraughin** picking thro' the furze and
  heather,
When I nearly fell across him, he was lying there so
  still;
  And we roamed the Summer evening together.

You remember that same night, too, happened Mary
  Carthy's spree,
  'Fore she went to learn dress-making off to Dublin;

---

* *Fraughin*, the Bilberry.

And, in spite of all my frowning, the whole time he
    kept by me—
    Sure, 'tis often since that thought myself was
        troublin'!
How, old Simon Carroll cried, as we both danced "The
    Spauladore":
    "Arrah, boys and girls! come now and see some
        dancing!"
And our Matty and your brother Paudh down for us
    hauled a door,
    Just to place beneath our feet so quickly glancing!

Oh! I grew ashamed to witness all the parish 'most
    around,
    That I nearly fainted at the dreadful notion;
But my Brian caught me tenderly before I touched
    the ground,
    And they said it was the heat and the commotion:
Then that plague of my whole lifetime, Cauthleen,
    Corny o' the Mill,
    With his eyes sharp as the foxes' crept anigh me—
Sure I thought of Brian *deelish* on the little heathy
    hill,
    And I vowed the *bodach* miller ne'er would buy
        me!

Well, unknown to even you dear, Brian met me many
    an eve
    In the knockeen 'yond' the rath of Coolnamanagh,

And last Sunday he besought me soon for him my
    home to leave,

But I said to tell my parents, Cauth alanna!

Then he said he heard my father long had threatened
    to him ill

If he dared to look at me, his promised daughter—

Oh! I spent a mournful evening 'neath the little
    heathy hill:

My own tears would nearly fill the Deereen water!

Then my father's face this morning than the turf more
    darkly grew,

While my mother like the "goundril bawn"* abused
    me—

She could never make out quite, dear, what her girl
    was coming to!

Till my father cried at last that she ill-used me!

Then, all sadly, Cauth, and bitterly he asked me if
    his will

To go marry Corny would not be regarded—

Ah! I pictured Brian leaping down the little heathy
    hill;

And my sobs his further questions off me warded!

---

* *Goundril bawn,* the gander, "beaten and abused like the
goundril bawn!" is a favourite country expression.

Ah! but Cauthaleen, what would you do this day,
  achorra bawn?

  You'd be true to him? God bless your heart, my
    girsha!

For although but poor, his love to me's as welcome
    as the dawn;

  Then his honest, pleading eyes—oh, *wirra
    wirsha!*

Sure, until my latest breath, Cauth, I will love my
    Brian still;

  And I'll bless that day when half asleep we found
    him,

As we went a *fraughin* picking on the little heathy
    hill;

  And we stood two laughing maidens all around
    him!

THE DAY OF THE FAIR.

(Air—O'Connell's Trip to Parliament," or "Tee-
totaller's Reel."—LEVY, page 16.)

AN INTERRUPTED MONOLOGUE.

"The pigs are in the creel, 'tis time to put the start
to them,

They ought to fetch a deal o' money when we're
partin' them;

The darlints how they squeal—they know where we
are cartin' them,

For Lady Day is come, an' the gale we have to pay!

Oh! hurry, Mike, me son, go put your Sunday *cau-
been* on,

The clock has just struck one, the road we should
have long been on;

An' put the hasp upon the gate, you careless
omadhaun,

We'll never raich Taghmon before the breakin' of
the day!

"I promised Mauria, shure, I would *not* taste the
  pottheen more,
She tould me to procure the makin's of a *cothamor* ;*
I hear that Tommy Poor has some good friezes got
  in store,
  For raley, Mickaleen, we two want some shuits of
  grey. . .
The creel is creakin' bad, we'll have to get the smith
  again,
The nuts that last he had were mortial loose for
  fittin' in—
Our mare — hurra, me lad! — can go without a
  whippin' in,
  We'll raich Taghmon, ay, long before the breakin'
  of the day!

 . . . .

"Good-mornin', honest man—what am I lookin'
  hither now?
As much shure, as I can—say seven pound the litther
  now!
Six poun'? Hould out your han'—we'll split the little
  differ now,
  An' clinch the bargain. Very good; so drive them
  all away!
Shure that was Matty Kehoe, a dacint man from
  Dublin town,
'Twas he that bought our sow, last Shroft, beyant in
  Maudlintown,

---

* *Cothamór*, an overcoat.

No nonsense he'll allow, the money he'll be shovellin'
down--

    An' so the pigs are canted at the breakin' of the
    day!

.   .   .   .   .   .

"How wer' ye, Misther Doyle?—you too have sowld
    your *bonneens* shure;

Is that you, Corney Coyle?—why now we're all at
    Commin's doore;

Come in an' chat awhile, I know you're aich a con-
    noishure,

    I'm only takin' wine—well, whatever else you say.

I wondher where's me boy—is that he buyin' ginger-
    bread

For Nelly M'Elroy?   Well, how that girl does fringe
    her head!

The frieze I think I'll buy—how dhrink does all un-
    hinge your head—

    I'm tastin' all the mornin' since the breakin' of the
    day!

"Three glasses now I've took, but Mauria wouldn't
    notice it,

I'll swear upon The Book, the sorra drop I got as
    yet;

An' innocent I'll look upon her sittin' opposite,

    While she says: 'Wisha, shure, I knew that same
    would be the way!'

I'll say I'm almost drown'd, to keep her long tongue
off o' me—

I'll mention seven pound an' then she'll never scoff at
me ;

So turn the mare around, 'tis time, I think, we off
should be,

We're long enough here gosth'ring, since the
breakin' of the day !"

THE DANCE AT MARLEY.

Murtagh Murphy's barn was full to the door, when
eve grew dull,

    For Phelim Moore his beautiful new pipes had
brought to charm them;

In the kitchen thronged the girls—cheeks of roses,
teeth of pearls!

    Admiring bows, and braids, and curls, till Phelim's
notes alarmed them.

Quick each maid her hat and shawl hung on dresser,
bed, or wall,

    Smoothed down her hair and smiled on all, as she
the bawnoge* entered;

Where a shass† of straw was laid on a ladder, raised,
that made

    A seat for them, as still they stayed, while dancers
by them cantered.

---

* *Bawnogue,* a dance floor.   † *Shass,* a bundle (seat).

Murtagh and his Vanithee had their chairs brought in
  to see

  The heels and toes go fast and free, and fun and
    love and laughter ;

In their sconces all alight shone the tallow candles
  bright—

  The flames kept jigging all the night, upleaping to
    the rafter !

The pipes, with noisy, drumming sound, every lover's
  whispering drowned,

  So the couples took their ground—their hearts
    within them dancing !

Merrily, with toe and heel, airily in jig and reel,

  Fast in and out they whirl and wheel, all capering
    and prancing.

"Off she Goes," "The Rocky Road," "The Tipsy
  House," and "Miss M'Cloud,"

  "The Devil's Dream," and "Jig Polthogue," "The
    Wind that Shakes the Barley;"

"The First o' May," "The Garran Buee," "Tatter
  Jack Walsh," "The River Lee"—

  As lapping breakers from the sea the myriad tunes
    at Marley !

Reels of three and reels of four, hornpipes and jigs
  galore,

  With singles, doubles held the floor in turn, without
    a bar low ;

But when fun and courting lulled, and the dancing
somewhat dulled,
The door unhinged the boys down pulled, for
" Follow me up to Carlow."

Ned and Nelly, hand in hand, footed in a square so
grand,
Then back the jingling door they spanned, and
swept swift as their glances.
Ned, indignant-like, retired, chased by Nell, until he
tired,
And her constancy admired, that he soon made
advances.
But young Nell would not be won, and a lover's chase
came on—
The maidens laughed to see the fun, till she sur-
rendered fairly :
Hands enclasped in rosy pride, tripping neatly, side
by side,
They turned and bowed most dignified to all the
folk of Marley !

Poorly pen of sage or scribe could such scenes of joy
describe,
Or due praises fair ascribe, where all were nearly
equal !
The love-making I've forgot in each cozy *saustagh**
spot—
Yet now I think I'd better not go tell, but wait the
sequel.

---

* *Saustagh,* comfortable.

Everything must have an end, and the *girshas** homewards wend,

   With guarding brother and a friend—this last
was absent rarely!

Late the Murphys by the hearth talked about their
evening's mirth—

   Ne'er a dance upon the earth could match their
own at Marley!

---

* *Girshas,* girls.

Miscellaneous Songs.

——◆——

EVAL FROM THE FAYLANDS.

(A Fairy Legend.)

From the western Faylands, Eval, o'er the billow
Drove her swan, Finala, till her mystic willow
    Touched the breathing vessel, when the sands lay
      bare,
    Changing tre sea skimmer, to a prancing mare.
Sought, the blushing Eval, one to share her pillow,
    Kiss her curvèd forehead, twine her flowing hair.

By thy star-pierced hillock, Loran Rhu, snow
    wreathèd,
Pined the minstrel Cahal, with no harp that
    breathèd:
    Bardic wrath and anger, thundering, he hurled—
    Fiery aoirs and satires on a songless world;
Curse and malediction, through his grey lips, seethèd,
    On the harpless banner, o'er the land unfurled.

Stark and rigid, by him, stretched the wings, broad-
shouldered,
  Of a gaunt blue bittern on a border, bouldered:
    Mute, its beak, wide gaping, told of dearth and
    drought,
    Of the ice-barred rivers, and their prisoned trout,
  Of a wan, wide prospect, where a lone heart
  mouldered,
    Till its frozen spirit scarce could issue out!

    .   .   .   .   .   .

Eval from the Faylands, rode with radiant figure,
Like a star, fanned brightest by the North wind's
  vigour.
  Swiftly o'er the snow flakes glittering, she sped
  Noiseless as a halcyon o'er a river bed;
Till she reached the outcast, spent with cold and
  rigour,
  On the white snow resting his wild, throbbing head.

" Rise, poor harpless minstrel—soft, but chill thy
  pillow!—
Snow?" she gently questioned; as amid the billow,
  'Bove her palfrey's bridle, fair, her fingers peeped,
  Like a range of sea gulls, in the briny steeped;
Then, she touched his eyelids with her mystic willow,
  And their fettered glances, loosened, to her
  leaped!

"Lo, the star of evening," sighed the minstrel, see-
    ing:
"From its blue cirque swerving, slips into my being!
    Tell me, what, O Princess! seekest thou of me—
    O'er the world's rim, travelling, I would roam for
      thee?"
"Come," said Western Eval—"come and leave thy
    dreeing—
    Minstrel of my bosom! o'er the drumming sea!"

Over hill and valley, fleet their palfrey pranced;
Over wave and billow swift their cygnet glanced;
    Till they reached a palace, set in sunny zone,
    Shut with bronzen portal, domed with diamond
      stone;
Wonderstruck, the minstrel gazed with eyes en-
    tranced,
    On its pleasures opening to her queenly tone!

    .   .   .   .   .

Thronged the happy harpers of her Isle of Pleasure,
That eve to their presence, trolling many a measure;
    Varied, with each minstrel, as his haunt and race:
    One, from the smooth liosses, sang of feasts and
      plays;
One, from ocean caverns, of immortal leisure;
    One, from hunting bothy, of the headlong chase!

H

Sang, till Cahal wistful grew their lays to share in;

As his memory wandered to the plains of Érinn.

> Brought, each chaunt of hunting, chief and deer and hound;

> Brought, each festive chorus, wine and music's sound;

Brought, each cavern echo, many a chieftain's cairn—

Many a bardic mansion, levelled to the ground!

Till the fairy music from his heart went, grieving;

For its welcomer tarried, other guests receiving:

> Érinn's many harpers—winds and waters—made

> Merry in his mem'ry,—heard alone, they played,

Till like threadless shuttle, ceased the clairseach's weaving,

> Then, young Eval, guessing his heart longing, said:

"Take my harp, dear Cahal, sing a lay of courting,

A true lover's legend, meet for us, disporting:

> Over sea in Érinn, ye have one, that yet

> Lingers with its harpers, though their sun hath set—

Oisin and his Niav, centuries consorting—

> Parted then:" she gazing, saw his eyes were wet!

As he tuned her clairseach, listened her fair legions;
But no lay of Érinn filled the fairy regions—
  'Twas a lover's lyric, praising her sweet grace,
  Who had wiled the minstrel to this pleasant place;
But he ceased his rapture, for his voice obedience
  Paid her hand, eclipsing half her blushing face.

"None but harp of Érinn," sighed the bard, "can
    borrow
Strains to match that legend, tuned to earthly
    sorrow!—
  I will take thy cygnet, journey to my land,
  Smite the yew and willow; then, with crafty hand,
I will shape a harp frame, string with gold chords
    thorough;
  Then, returning hither, love, thou cans't com-
    mand!"

As upon the cygnet, Cahal stood, young Eval,
Her long willow gave him, saying: "Ocean devil
  Cannot hurt nor harm thee, while thy pinioned sail
  Screens from clutching danger, tooth, and claw,
    and tail;
But, apast the billows, fear earth foes, uncivil,
  Swan for palfrey changing ride o'er hill and
    dale."

" Fare-thee-well, sweet Eval !"—" Fare-thee-well, dear
    rover !
" Now Finala, safely bring me back my lover !"
    And the cygnet hearing, bent a pliant bow,
    Gliding o'er the ocean, till, a speck of snow
Hung upon the sea line; then it toppled over,
    Like a flower, a moment above a water flow !

.   .   .   .   .

Came the eastering minstrel o'er the seas, blue
    braided,
From the Faylands speeding, till its glory faded;
    Then he heard the green waves laughing, soft and
    bland,
    At the white spray gambols o'er the level sand—
Thence, he ploughed a passage, arrowy and bladed,
    Touching port and refuge on a silver strand !

Lo, as on his vision, burst the hills of Eri—
Peak and passage mantled, snowy-bright and
    glary,
    Thoughts tumultuous crowding, thronged his eager
    brain,
    Full of restless longing for the promised strain,
When his native clairseach, strung for his dear fairy,
    He would wake to music once and sweet
    again !

Wand in hand, he bounded from the sea's surcingle,
Fast across the sand bars, faster o'er the shingle,
　　Hearing not Finala snorting by the tide—
　　Heeding not her white wings flapping wild and
　　　wide:
Till, dark interpacing many a distant dingle,
　　Sought he for the willow and the yew, allied.

Waited, vain, the cygnet by the sea's dominions,
Shuffling the wet night mist from her darkened
　　pinions,
　　Till the dawn wind ushered morning, overland,
　　Whose gold eye surpiercing wooded hill and strand,
'Found a harper, murdered by the King's harsh
　　minions,
　　Clasping a white willow in his frigid hand !

HALLOWE'EN.

Let us hasten, little stóireen!
  Listen, darling; Shep is snarling,
Seeing down the rugged bóreen
    Slua-Shee* sweeping through the air,
O'er the bogland's matted rushes,
'Yond the mountain's prickly bushes,
  To the moonshine—fairy sunshine—
    Of the liosses, grey and bare!

Whitely, o'er the haunted hill-path,
  See the curling dust goes whirling—
To the dewy-mantled cill-rath
    Haste the Shee this Hallowe'en—
Should they meet thee, they would take thee,
And their lowly menial make thee—
  Slippers mending, work unending,
    For the little man in green!

---

* The Fairy Host.

Once, I knew a tiny fellow,
  Darksome straying, out a-playing,
He, amid the traneens yellow,
  Lay a tired, benighted youth;
Then a bubble-eyed arch-luchre,
Tipped with steely spots and ochre,
  Sudden, rising, leaped surprising,
    Clean adown his wondering mouth!

Now, the Luricaun roams, bedless—
  He's a fairy, sly and wary!
And the Dulicaun comes headless,
  Seeking for some other one.
His long arms are ever sweeping,
Till they touch some stranger, sleeping,
  Who awakes, and moaning makes—
    For his head, for ever gone!

Fear, astor, the fire fringed Shee-rings,
  Never venture them to enter;
Ended, else thy field journeyings—
  Withered, shrunken grown, and wan;
While the fairy poochas, grazing,
At their stunted cowherd gazing,
  Would keep saying—"Ceased thy straying,
    Now, my little whey-faced man!"

Now, at last, thou growest fearful,
　　Of, my dearie, things so eerie;
But, my darling, be not tearful—
　　Cross thyself, and they are gone;
For the Slua-Shee cannot charm thee,
Nor their magic hurt or harm thee:
　　Two things be, which fairies flee—
　　Evening prayer and morning sun!

MY BEAUTIFUL MARY O!

(Air in Joyce's *Irish Music and Song*, p. 17.)

The drifted snow clings to the brow of the mountain,
    to-night,
And purely it glistens in peace, 'neath the moon's
    silvery light;
But whiter and brighter than sheen of the moon on
    the snow
Is the brow of my darling—my beautiful Mary O!

Oh, leave the way, lovers!—to all is her heart tightly
    locked;
There, once, faint and trembling, a suitor, I wistfully
    knocked;
But, sweet was my welcome—such welcome but few
    lovers know,
That sprang from the lips of my beautiful Mary O!

Ah, she is the gentlest of maidens, that ever gave
    love,
As pure as the angels, that rustle with white wings
    above—

A love, that makes for me, a heaven of earth here
  below,

Lit by the bright eyes of my beautiful Mary O!

I hear her clear laugh, when a pebble I drop in the
  well;

I hear her low voice, in the murmur of sea-parted
  shell;

I hear her love sigh, in the plaint of the breezes that
  blow,

Returning with mine, to my beautiful Mary O!

The lake is not burthened, though holding a swan or
  its breast;

The hill feels not heavy, the snow shining white on
  its crest;

And so her rare beauty, that sets all my breast in
  a glow,

Lies light on the heart of my beautiful Mary O!

Oh, nine times a day, goes my heart o'er the mountains to her,

By love, swiftly pinioned, a tireless and true
  messenger,

Till in the near future, the same southward path I
  will go,

To claim my heart's darling—my beautiful Mary O!

THE BONNIE BROWN-HAIRED GIRL WHOM I LOVE.

(Air—"The Fair Hills of Ireland.")

(Uileacán Dubh O !)

Ah! God be with the mornings, when my love and I
    went Maying,
    Through the silent, heathery Glen of Imayle;
When the dawn o'er Lugnaquila, like a fairy host
    arraying,
    Chased the flying elves of night, down the vale!
Still, the fairies peep and play, on this twinkling May
    Day—
Still the elfin bands sink vanishing, before the bright
    array;
But, alas! my sweet maiden is far, far away—
    The bonnie brown-haired girl, whom I love!

A hundred thousand welcomes, love, you gave me,
    slowly going,
    Through the silent, heathery Glen of Imayle:
How I cherished them and treasured them, till, surer,
    poorer growing,
    I wandered to the town from the vale. .

Could you know, O my fond one! my long nights of
    pain—

Could you feel, O my dear one! my heart's constant
    strain,

There, toiling and moiling, bright riches to gain,

    For the bonnie brown-haired girl, whom I love!

Alas, my love, one Patrick's morn, sailed swift across
    the billow,

    From the silent, heathery Glen of Imayle;

And I am all alone, each night, with sorrow for my
    pillow,

    Far away from my own native vale!

Love of loves—O, my love! could you hear my sad
    moan,

You would never, never leave me in Ireland, alone,

To sigh and to cry, morn and evening—ochon!—

    For the bonnie brown-haired girl, whom I love!

'Tis true, your lover, my brown girl!—was poor in
    earthly treasure,

    In the silent, heathery Glen of Imayle!

'Tis true, your lover, my brown girl!—with mingled
    pain and pleasure,

    To win you riches, went from the vale.

But, mo-nuar! O mo-nuar! when the bright wealth
   had come,
Then, mo-nuar! O mo-nuar! you had left your moun-
   tain home—
Ah, my heart, this sad morning, flies over the foam,
  To the bonnie, brown-haired girl, whom I love!

Oh, rare you are, and fair you are, as ever ring of
   morning,
  'Bove the silent, heathery Glen of Imayle;
And mild you are, and kind you are, God's choicest
   gifts adorning
  The pride of our own native vale:
And I go now to seek you, for a year and a day,
Till I find you and bind you close to my side, alway,
To enfold and to hold, till I'm stretched in the clay,
  The bonnie brown-haired girl, whom I love!

THE HOUSE IN THE CORNER.

(Air in R. M. Levy's Collection, page 15.)

It stood like a hive at the bend of the lane,
  Where trumans and quickens formed guardians
    around;
It laughed at the sun, and it smiled at the rain;
  And it winked at the tempest that fretted and
    frowned.
Oh! my bright little cabin, my white little cabin,
  So blithesome and cheery, so lightsome and airy!
When Death some fine day will come, haunting me
    troublesome,
  The house in the corner I'll first have to see!

Oh! thither came Robin when evening drew nigh,
  Enthroned on his branch, how his red bosom
    heaved,
With a full fluttering throat, and delirious eye,
  He sang for us all, whether blest or bereaved,

In the bright little cabin, the white little cabin,
  So blithesome and cheery, so lightsome and airy!
When Death some fine day will come, haunting me
    troublesome,
  The house in the corner I'll first have to see!

But sweeter, I trow, out from window and door,
  And softer the song that all tremulous swelled,
When Mary's fresh voice like a harp clear would
    pour,
  That Robin grew mute, for his strain was excelled,
In the bright little cabin, the white little cabin,
  So blithesome and cheery, so lightsome and airy!
When Death some fine day will come, haunting me
    troublesome,
  The house in the corner I'll first have to see!

Ah! Mary *astor*, of these evenings I think,
  When you and red Robineen emulous strove;
But now at the thought doth my heart sadly sink,
  For Robin is mated, and I'm from my love,
And the bright little cabin, the white little cabin,
  So blithesome and cheery, so lightsome and airy,
When Death some fine day will come, haunting me
    troublesome,
  The house in the corner I'll first have to see!

CREEVEEN CNO.*
(An Irish Cradle Song.)

I will sing a queer song for my Creeveen Cno,
That I heard from a fairyman long ago;
Beneath a red rowan he hammered away
And lilted a song all the summer day—
      O ho! dear, shall we go
      O ho! all in a row,
  To see a strange palace, as fair as a chalice,
      With a cradle of gold for my Creeveen Cno?

He sang: "I've a mansion, as round as the sun,
In the mossy rath, hidden from everyone;
'Tis guarded by thrushes, brown speckled and bright,
That sing in their sleep in the hush of the night!"—
      O ho! dear, shall we go—
      O ho! all in a row,
  To see the bold thrushes stand guard on the bushes
      And fifing up music for Creeveen Cno?

---

* Little branch or cluster of nuts—a pet name for a child.

"My sister's a nightingale out in the wood;
My brother's a drummer for Conn the Good;
My father's a gentleman, snug in his chair;
My mother's a dealer in china ware!"—
        O ho! dear, shall we go—
        O ho! all in a row?
    His father and mother, his sister and brother
            Have millions of kisses for Creeveen Cno!

"I've a dandy grey mare and a pussy cat brown,
And a mouse brings me oatenmeal out of the town.
A little white rabbit sleeps high on my knee,
And a robin picks all the bright berries for me!"—
        O ho! dear, shall we go—
        O ho! all in a row,
    A dish of strawberries, raspberries, and cherries,
            Red Robin has ready for Creeveen Cno!

"There is bread in the cupboard, and cheese on the
        shelf;
And if you want more you can get it yourself—
A bit for old Peter, a bit for young Paul,
And a bit for the beggar outside the wall!"—
        O ho! dear, shall we go—
        O ho! all in a row?
    This sweet bread and butter will make a nice
        supper
            For good little children like Creeveen Cno!

I

" My butler's a gander, grey-feathered and fat,
Who wears a blue jacket and three-cocked hat ;
His wife often pecks him—he gravely will prance
When to please the young goslins, she bids him to
    dance !"—
        O ho ! dear, shall we go—
        O ho ! all in a row ?
This foolish old gander will to the moor wander
        To jig for my good little Creeveen Cno !

" I've a black-coated coachman, a dog called Ruff,
And I sent him to town for a pinch of snuff,
He broke my box and he spilled my snuff !"—
Then the man said his story was long enough !
        O ho ! dear, shall we go—
        O ho ! all in a row ?
Be sure, when I'm buried and you, love, are
    married,
        In heaven I'll watch o'er my Creeveen Cno !

THE BONNIE CUCKOO.

(Air in Bunting.)

When riding from Town, on the First o' May,
  A-down by the river, I lost my purse!
    Asthrue! Asthrue! O, cooing cuckoo,
  So bright and so blue!—it was full, of course:
    So true, 'tis true, my bonnie cuckoo!—
  My fortune, that evening, could not be worse.

So, going, a-seeking that First o' May,
  A-down by the river, 'mid heath and furze—
    Arue! arue! O, cooing cuckoo!
  So bright and so blue!—sure, I got my purse!
    'Tis true for you, my bonnie cuckoo!—
  I gave the fair finder a kiss, of course!

Now, coming from Town, on this last o' May,
  Along by the river, I ride my horse—
    Achue! achue! O, cooing cuckoo!
  So bright and so blue!—now my loss is worse!—
    'Tis true, too true, my bonnie cuckoo!—
  My heart I must find where I found my purse!

THE BLACKBIRD AND THE THRUSH.

(Air in Davidson's *Irish Melodies*, page 57.)

Why, O why, O why, glossy blackbird,
  Sit ye, silent, high above the leaves,
While the sun is dawning on
    The ploughlands of the eastern waves?

I am silent, yellow speckled thrush,
  For I see the red lark in the sky
Sowing grains of happy strains
    For my reaping—that's the why—O why! O why!

Why, O why, O why, glossy blackbird,
  Sit ye, singing, hid among the leaves,
While the sun is setting on
    The cornfields of the Western waves?

I am singing, yellow-speckled thrush,
  For the seeds the red lark sowed on high,
Seven fold, with bill of gold,
    I am reaping—that's the why, O why! O why!

NO, NO, NOT I.

'Neath lofty Mount Leinster my true lover dwelt,
And one dewy evening beside me he knelt;
He asked me to wed him, but cold my reply,
As lightly I answered him—No, no—not I!
　　My dear, no, no—not I!

Like a sea mist, enshrouding the stars in the skies,
A haze dimmed the lovelight that shone in his eyes;
As blinded with grief, forth he went with a sigh—
His lonesome heart echoing—No, no—not I!
　　My dear, no, no—not I!

My own little sister beheld his strange look,
In the wood, hardly knowing what pathway he took—
O sister, dear sister, how did you reply?
And lightly I answered her—No, no—not I!
　　My dear, no, no—not I!

My brother frowned darkly, my father looked grave;
And my mother no moments of peace to me gave—
Is it true that the lover, who for you would die,
You spurned with the cruel words—No, no—not I!
　　My dear, no, no—not I!

But vain was their chiding, till Sunday came on,
When, going the Mass-path, I heard he had gone;
He had sailed o'er the salt seas, nor left a good-bye,
To the false maid who answered him—No, no,—not I!
My dear, no, no—not I!

The news like white lightning my heart split in two,
For I loved him!—I loved him! oh, what would I do?
No Mass could I hear, but I crept home to lie,
On a fever bed, moaning my—No, no—not I!
My dear, no, no—not I!

I sigh, when I go the Mass-path, where we walked;
I cry when I sit 'neath the oak, where we talked;
'Twould be blest relief, if I only could die,
To still the sad echo of—No, no—not I!
My dear, no, no—not I!

I will take a small bag, and a-begging I'll go,
O'er hedges and ditches, all covered with snow;
And when I am weary I'll sit down and cry,
And rue the first day I said—No, no—not I!
My dear, no, no—not I!*

---

* This stanza belongs to an old country song, and is the
only verse I could discover which survives.

SYMPATHY.

Wherefore, O Bard! 'mid the rush and roar
  Of the world's struggle, so fierce and vain,
Where ears are dulled, and where hearts no more
  Delight in aught but in greed and gain,
Should'st thou the songs of thy heart outpour,
  In such blitheful vein?

   .   .   .   .   .

Mounteth a form from the meadow's heart—
  A wee brown bird that sings up the skies,
Waking a student with dreamy start;
  Yet smileth his face, grown white and wise;
This song that soothes with such magic art
  Is a glad surprise!

Riseth a bud in a city room,
  Casting the green hood from 'round its head;
Yet never a one may praise its bloom,
  Save the dying girl on her weary bed;
But O her great joy that it has come,
  Ere she lay dead!

Droppeth some gold on the waste of snow—
  A sunbeam that creeps up the lover's path;
Yet not one blossom it sees, and so
  It climbs to a ruby throne that hath
Begun on a robin's bosom to blow—
  A rose-aftermath!

Lispeth a lip some endearing word;
  It is noon of night and the small one dreams
Of a new, strange world of bud and bird,
  And of golden sand in the whisp'ring streams—
By all save the mother's ear unheard.
  Ah! she sleepless seems!

.   .   .   .

So, thou can'st find from the rush and roar
  Of the human conflict, raging 'round,
Some lonely spot where a heart is sore—
  Where grief or care hath a foothold found!
Be it so; sing, good minstrel, ever more,
  Till thou'rt glory-crowned!

www.ingramcontent.com/pod-product-compliance
Lightning Source LLC
Chambersburg PA
CBHW030607270326
41927CB00007B/1083